William James
and the Reinstatement
of the Vague

William James
and the Reinstatement
of the Vague

WILLIAM JOSEPH GAVIN

TEMPLE UNIVERSITY PRESS
Philadelphia

Temple University Press, Philadelphia 19122
Copyright © 1992 by Temple University. All rights reserved
Published 1992
Printed in the United States of America

Library of Congress Cataloging-in-Publication Data

Gavin, William Joseph, 1943–
William James and the reinstatement of the vague / William Joseph
Gavin.
p.   cm.
Includes bibliographical references and index.
ISBN 0-87722-946-5 (alk. paper)
1. James, William, 1842–1910.   2. Vagueness (Philosophy)—
History—20th century.   I. Title.
B945.J24G38   1992
191—dc20
                                                    91-32387

For Cathy

Our mind is so wedded to the process of seeing an other *beside every item of its experience, that when the notion of an absolute datum is presented to it, it goes through its usual procedure and remains pointing at the void beyond.*
"The Sentiment of Rationality"

As long as one continues talking, *intellectualism remains in undisturbed possession of the field. The return to life can't come about by talking. It is an* act; *to make you return to life, I must set an example for your imitation. I must deafen you to talk . . . by showing you . . . that the concepts we talk with are made for purposes of* practice *and not for the purposes of insight. Or I must* point, *point to the mere* that *of life, and you by inner sympathy must fill out the* what *for yourselves.*
A Pluralistic Universe

There is no conclusion. What has concluded, that we might conclude in regard to it?
"A Suggestion about Mysticism"

Contents

Contents

PART THREE
APPLICATIONS

Acknowledgments

John J. McDermott of Texas A & M University first introduced me to William James and to the importance of "the vague" several years ago. At that time he and Robert Pollock, another influence, were synonymous with the term "American Philosophy" at Fordham University. John E. Smith and Maurice Natanson of Yale University both read several chapters of the text in an earlier version. Tom Rockmore of Duquesne University has been particularly helpful in offering encouragement and support for the project, as well as reading several of the chapters. For more than two decades, students in the Philosophy Department and more recently in the Honors Program at the University of Southern Maine have responded with kind enthusiasm to my efforts to teach James. No doubt many of their helpful comments have found their way into the present text, and for this I am grateful. My secretary, John Corcoran, worked tirelessly to produce the final manuscript.

Jane Cullen, senior acquisitions editor at Temple University Press, has been a joy to work with, offering both continual support and helpful criticism of the manuscript. Two anonymous reviewers for the Press offered extremely helpful comments on an earlier draft of this text. Their constructive criticisms have served to make the present volume a much stronger one. Jennifer French, production editor, provided constant assistance throughout the entire process. Finally, the book is dedicated to my wife, Cathy, who, once again, has encouraged me to believe in my dreams.

I am grateful to the following publishers for granting permission to reprint the following articles, either in whole or in part and with revisions:

"William James and the Importance of 'The Vague,'" *Cultural Hermeneutics* 3, no. 3 (March 1976), pp. 245–65.

"William James, Dieu, et la possibilité actuelle," *Archives de Philosophie*, Tome 52, Cahier 4 (Octobre–Décembre 1989), pp. 529–38. Courtesy of Beauchesne Publishers.

"Panthéisme pluraliste et possibilité actuelle: Réflexions sur *A Pluralistic Universe* de William James," *Archives de Philosophie*, Tome 47, Cahier 4 (Octobre–Décembre 1984), pp. 557–68. Courtesy of Beauchesne Publishers.

"William James' Philosophy of Science," *New Scholasticism* 52, no. 3 (Summer 1978), pp. 413–20. Courtesy of the American Catholic Philosophical Association.

"William James and the Indeterminacy of Language and 'The Really Real,'" *Proceedings of the American Catholic Philosophical Association* 50 (1976), pp. 208–18.

"William James on Language," *International Philosophical Quarterly* 16, no. 1 (March 1976), pp. 81–86.

"James' Metaphysics: Language as the House of 'Pure Experience,'" *Man and World* 12, no. 2 (1979), pp. 142–59. Courtesy of Kluwer Academic Publishers.

"Peirce and 'The Will to Believe,'" *The Monist* 63, no. 3 (July 1980), pp. 342–50.

"Text, Context, and the Existential Limit: A Jamesian Strain in Marx and Dewey," in *Context over Foundation: Dewey and Marx*, edited by William J. Gavin (Dordrecht: D. Reidel Publishing Co., 1988), pp. 49–73. Courtesy of Kluwer Academic Publishers.

"Modern Art and William James," *Science/Technology & the Humanities* 1, no. 1 (Winter 1978), pp. 45–54.

"Vagueness and Empathy: A Jamesian View," *Journal of Medicine and Philosophy* 6, no. 1 (February 1981), pp. 45–65. Courtesy of Kluwer Academic Publishers.

"William James and the Need to Preserve 'the Vague,' " Walter E. Russell Lecture, University of Southern Maine, 1986.

Introduction

Why "the Vague"?

In *The Principles of Psychology*, the American philosopher William James makes what at first sight appears as a strange statement. He tells the reader: "It is, in short, the re-instatement of the vague to its proper place in our mental life which I am so anxious to press on the attention."[1] Furthermore, this type of reference is by no means an isolated one in the Jamesian corpus. In "The Will to Believe," he says: "In the great boarding-house of nature, the cakes and the butter and the syrup seldom come out . . . even and leave the plates . . . clean. Indeed we should view them with scientific suspicion if they did."[2] In *Pragmatism*, he tells the reader, "Profusion, not economy, may after all be reality's key-note"[3]; and asks: "May there not after all be a possible ambiguity in truth?"[4] And in *Essays in Radical Empiricism*, he calls "our experiences, taken all together, a quasi-chaos."[5] Now most philosophers, and indeed most people, do not set out to emphasize the vague. Quite the opposite: most have pursued certainty, objectivity, and some form of universal truth. Furthermore, most have assumed that such truth can be captured in language, that is, that a complete linguistic description of reality is at least possible, and certainly desirable. Yet James does not. He specifically lashes out at what he calls "vicious intellectualism," which, he says, consists in the *"treating of a name as excluding from the fact named what the name's definition fails positively to include."*[6] And in *Psychology (Briefer Course)*, he is even more radical, telling the reader that it is "the reinstatement of the vague *and inarticulate* to its proper place" that he wants so anxiously to emphasize.[7]

A word of caution is necessary at this stage. James does not use the term "vague" in its usual pejorative sense, nor does he employ any singular term like "vague" throughout his writings. Indeed, as some of the quotations above indicate, he is much more the master of diverse concrete imagery and analogy and, as we shall see below, suspicious of the usurping of too much power by conceptual theory and linguistic terminology. Nonetheless, he does employ this term in a central chapter of *The Principles of Psychology*. Furthermore, the crucial aspects of the term "vagueness," that is, the "richness" and "intensity" of life, can be developed, and this task is undertaken at the beginning of Chapter One. For the present, it is important to note that the term "vague" is being used in these chapters not simply in a literal sense, but in more of a symbolic one, as an interpretative disclosure of James's overall outlook. Therefore, when one talks about the need to preserve the vague, or to nurture as "fat" or thick a context for our experiences as possible, this sense of vagueness should be distinguished from situations that I shall term "bumbling." At first glance, the two situations may look the same, but they are diametrically opposed, though often hard to tell apart. When James talks of the need to preserve the vague, he is arguing against certainty, that is, against the usurping of the privileged position of center stage once and for all by any formulation of the universe. His outlook is pluralistic, contextual, and multidimensional. "Bumbling" is a term I shall use to refer to a situation wherein one seeks certainty, seeks the apodictic, the fundamental Archimedean point as a necessary desideratum in life, but *fails* to find it. Bumbling, then, refers to a depressing state of affairs in which one allows the goal to be defined in terms of certainty and then cannot manage to achieve it—or at least to pretend to have achieved it. The vague, in contrast, refers to a situation that has not degenerated into an overly false clarity, and to one that does not intend to come up with final certainty. As Eugene Fontinell has put it:

> James's desire to reinstate the "vague and inarticulate" is . . . not a defense of obfuscation or romantic cloudiness. Paradoxically, it is an effort to describe our experience as rigorously as possible and to avoid any procrustean cutting of experience so as to fit neatly into what can be named or conceptualized. . . . This in no way denies the legitimacy and even necessity of extrapolating from or speculating upon our personal experiences. It does, however, caution against explaining away that which is present in our immediate experience.[8]

Vagueness in James has several dimensions, including but not limited to the personal, psychological, religious, epistemic, metaphysical, and even the textual. Its closest parallel outside the American tradition can be found in the works of Gabriel Marcel, who distinguished between a "problem" and a "mystery."[9] Problems are items that lie across my path; in raising questions about problems, I do not raise questions about my own existence, since I am not involved with the situation or context. Problems, such as quadratic equations or crossword puzzles, can be solved, and it does not really matter who solves them. A mystery, by contrast, is a problem that encroaches on its own data. In raising questions about mysteries, I also question myself, since I am part of the context, and so on. Most important for Marcel, what *appears* to exist are problems; what *really* exists are mysteries. My body is not a problem but a mystery; other people should be viewed as mysterious; God is not a "great geometer" à la Galileo but an ultimate mystery. "Being" or "reality" is not something we solve, but rather something we "attest to" or have faith in. While James would extend the domain of the "mysterious" or, in his terms, the "vague" even further to include aspects of nature, and even of science, he surely would have agreed with Marcel's overall stance here.

James's position on the "inarticulate" can be made clearer by contrasting it with that of his contemporary in American philosophy, Charles Sanders Peirce, who also nurtured an appreciation for vagueness. Peirce charged that "logicians have too much neglected the study of *vagueness*," and in opposition to this he says, "I have worked out the logic of vagueness with something like completeness." [10] But to James, a philosopher who found the universe to be "wild—game-flavored as a hawk's wing," [11] and who held that "ever not quite" [12] trails along after any philosopher's *interpretation* of reality, the temptation to "clean up" the vague, though a strong one, would nonetheless have been extremely alarming. But the issue is a difficult one. How can one be articulate about the inarticulate, or clear about the vague, without undermining or "explaining away" what it is that one wants to preserve? On the one hand, one cannot just work up a theory of vagueness. On the other hand, one cannot simply dismiss theory or language altogether. As James himself realized, theories are to be judged pragmatically, in terms of their leadings. Theories, or languages, are *directional*, and not exclusively descriptive. But they are not dismissable—"neo-pragmatism" to the contrary. Frank Lentricchia gives voice to this necessity by telling the reader:

> One cannot "try" or "not try" to be a theorist. Theory is not simply a matter of intention or will or conscious agency. It is a matter of necessity; an impulse, an appetite. . . . Theory—whether we call it structuralism or capitalism—is the desire which would be the "remedy" of difference. It cannot be dismissed. It can, however, be guarded against, and the method of vigilance is James's pragmatism. . . . But pragmatism (the vigilante within) is always on the verge of vanquishment, of giving belief over to theory (the totalitarian within). [13]

Lentricchia is indeed correct here, although James would want to emphasize a bit more the distinction between "vague intentions" and "intentions fulfilled" in, for example, having an idea of Memorial Hall and using the idea as a leading function actually to find the Hall that one then realizes one had "in mind."[14] Equally important, I will argue that the theme of "vague intentions" should be applied to James's *own texts*. They too, at a metatheoretical level, are interpreted in the essays that follow as directional signs and not as mere descriptions.

One should recall that the last book James wrote, *Some Problems of Philosophy*, has as its subtitle "The *Beginning* of an *Introduction* to Philosophy." James died with his somewhat systematic book "stopped in the middle of an arch." One wonders whether he was indeed capable of writing a finished text in philosophy, or whether his texts, like the outlooks they present, are not "vague" in the good sense of that term. As George Cotkin argues, "James's chances of ever completing a systematic philosophy in a rigorously technical style of expression, even without his popular presentations, remains debatable; systematization and technical presentation were not James's favored modes of philosophical exposition."[15] Lentricchia argues for a somewhat similar position when he tells the reader: "For the pragmatic textualist, who is the bibliographer's version of the devil, there is only one text: the forever unfinished, decentralized text of history—forever supplemented, new chapters being written in all sorts of places by all sorts of people not especially in touch with one another."[16] Lentricchia goes on to say, "There is no work of 'correspondence,' only of 'production.'"[17] While applauding the emphasis on creativity, James would have had difficulty accepting the exclusivity of these two concepts; he argued, for example, for "dynamic correspondence" in *Pragmatism*.

Going further, James's "originality" in offering a "fresh," that is, novel, text should not be confused with the fact that that text was supposed to reflect reality accurately, or more accurately than alternate texts—though apodictic proof was not to be thought of. Once again, the texts are to be seen as "directional"—pointing beyond themselves toward life in general. For this reason, while applauding the role of "vigilante," one should guard against any curtailment of its function exclusively to epistemology. I would offer as an alternative a broader reading of James, who, as Cornel West has noted, "promotes an Emersonian *evasion* of epistemology-centered philosophy."[18] That is, not only did James succeed in developing an antifoundationalist or a contextualist position; he also, for West, "preserves a realist ontology" that does not become preoccupied with an exclusive and elitist methodology. In my terminology, vagueness does indeed have an epistemic dimension, one that results in James's offering a methodology, that is, *Pragmatism*, which is suspicious of all formal systems, including itself. *Pragmatism* from a self-reflective perspective appears as epistemically vague, that is, appears as a hypothesis that must be tried out. But all vagueness is not epistemic vagueness; there are, for example, personal and textual dimensions to the vague.

The personal details of James's life are well known and need only be briefly referred to here. Never robust in health, James lost the use of his eyesight twice, suffered from insomnia and neurasthenia, and went through a serious personal conflict with nihilism in the late 1860s. Writing to his father from Berlin in 1867, he said: "Although I cannot exactly say that I got low-spirited, yet thoughts of the pistol, the dagger and the bowl began to usurp an unduly large part of my attention, and I began to think that some change, even if a hazardous one, was necessary."[19] This personal conflict with nihilism and subsequent temptation to commit suicide continues into 1870, when James "touches bottom" in February; by April of that year, however, he has read the works of Charles Renouvier and writes in his "diary": "I think that yesterday was a crisis in my life. I finished the second part of Renouvier's second 'Essais' and see no reason why his definition of Free Will—'the sustaining of a thought *because I choose to* when I might have other thoughts'—need be the definition of an illusion. . . . My first act of free will shall be to believe in free will. . . . Life shall [be built in] doing and suffering and creating." [20] The importance of this moment in the development of James's thought has been brought out by James scholars such as Ralph Barton Perry and John J. McDermott.[21] Furthermore, as Gerald Myers notes, it is not unique in nature.[22] It is important to realize that the issue James faced in 1868, sometimes prosaically referred to as the issue of freedom versus determinism, can best be framed in terms of vagueness. James realizes that he can marshal an argument for freedom and one for determinism. Both arguments are coherent and correspond to some available data. So the traditional categories of epistemology are inadequate to solve the problem. That is because it is not really a "problem" at all; rather does the issue appear phenomenologically as "mysterious" or as "vague," that is, open-textured and indeterminate. It is only because the issue is vague that James is compelled to take a stand, to commit himself to act. This personal or existential experience of the vague will receive its textual equivalent in "The Will to Believe"; but its metaphysical upshot is unclear until *A Pluralistic Universe*, and even then some problems remain.

Other commentators have unveiled different crises in James's life. Thus Daniel Bjork, in *William James: The Center of His Vision*, views a period between 1899 and 1902 as a time when James suffered a deep depression, "perhaps even more severe" [23] than the melancholia of 1868–69. James had irreparably strained his heart while walking in the mountains of Keene Valley, New York, in 1898. Ironically, as another commentator, Cushing Strout, has noted, it was only at this precise time that James had decided, with some fear and trembling, to cast off the career in science promoted by his father as a replacement for William's interest in art. Strout notes that James had even indicated an early interest in philosophy but had repressed it. But now,

at the age of fifty-seven James was at last prepared, with some trepidation, to give his full attention to those philosophical issues which had defined his ambition at the age of twenty-three. Suffering from a valvular lesion of the heart, he then spent six years trying to resign from Harvard. Four years after his resignation he died, convinced that his philosophy was "too much like an arch built only on one side." Nearly all his major philosophical work . . . began when he thought his professional career was finished.[24]

According to Bjork's interpretation, James tried to deal with this second crisis in the same way as he did the first one: by choosing an attitude, by redirecting and refocusing his vision. "Yet what worked in 1870 was not so workable in 1900. The active will was likely to be broken during a terminal illness."[25] While this is an insightful analysis, Bjork does not adequately realize that James's *texts*, that is, his *writings*, constitute an act of rebellion, or better, of aesthetic sublimation in a Nietzschean sense. This can be brought out by remembering that James's father had rebelled against his father (i.e., William's grandfather) by rejecting the God of Calvinism and embracing Swedenborg. Having done so, however, he did not extend the same option of free choice to his offspring, and William had some trouble "seeing" the path he was supposed to follow, since it tended to be inconsistent; William consequently became more "crippled," that is, dependent. His initial rebellion against determinism needed to be sustained, and it *was* sustained—through work, through activity, or more precisely, through the *text*. Strout catches this point nicely when he notes: "The elder James believed that men fell from grace individually, but could be saved collectively in a redeemed socialized society. His son, however, needed an individual salvation not only through faith but also in works. To translate this theological idiom, he needed to believe that there was point and purpose to some particular work of his own with social meaning. *He would finally save himself through his writing.*"[26] Bjork seems to realize but not to appreciate this same point about the text when he says that James "could not cancel his theoretical ambitions in exchange for the nirvana religious faith promised. . . . It was as if by moving, keeping busy, and remaining speculative he could evade the ontological reality religion met head on."[27] Bjork's interpretation of the 1898–1900 crisis relies too heavily on a biological/behavioral account of the "disease" and fails to see the text as an ongoing, though frail, act of rebellion that James managed to sustain almost up until the end of his life. Indeed, Bjork ends his work by introducing a new dualism, that is, by distinguishing "James's intellectual legacy . . . from the popular mythology about him. The James who defended will, choice, and action in the face of determinism and pessimism is the James who has persisted in the public mind. But the relational James, the James who tirelessly sought the essence of experience, is the James who has had the greater intellectual influence."[28] Such a distinction James would surely have found disconcerting, as it seems to obliterate any context wherein the fragile human self is at least sometimes creative. While the human self is indeed fragile and not Cartesian, James should not be viewed exclusively as a postmodernist,[29] and "the will to believe" is more important for his position than is often recognized.[30] But ironically, if Bjork's account, as its subtitle maintains, constitutes "the center of his (James's) vision," *he* (James) seems to have disappeared. By way of contrast, Ellen Kappy Suckiel, in her work *The Pragmatic Philosophy of William James*, says: "Our overview of James's philosophy has shown that the teleological subject—with his needs, desires, and interests—plays an indisputably central role in determining the character of the pragmatic world-view. A philosophy that eliminated reference to persons would be relegated to the realm of empty and remote intellectual abstractions having no true pertinence or value."[31] While this affirmation of the self is important, it underplays the fragility of the self both in James's life and in his theories. Fontinell offers a more detailed account of James's self, and one that stresses its fragility:

On the surface, James's doctrine of the self would seem to have developed through three stages. Beginning with a methodological dualism in his *Principles of Psychology*, James apparently moved to a "no-self" doctrine in the *Essays on Radical Empiricism*, and finally to the affirmation of a substantive self in *A Pluralistic Universe*. This three-stage view is basically sound and helpful as long as it is not understood as suggesting any clear, linear, and unequivocal development. In fact, there are tensions, shifts, inconsistencies, and even contradictions, not only between but also within these broad stages. Throughout, James is much less clear and confident about his positive affirmations and solutions than he is in describing the problems and what he wishes to avoid.[32]

The Jamesian self, then, is not reducible to something else, but neither can it be taken for granted as a finished product. Strout correctly suggests that James "had been a sick soul who became healthy minded through intellectual resistance to scientific and theological monism."[33] But even here the statement should be amended; whatever healthy-mindedness came through resistance was not a permanent ideal to be achieved once and for all at some point in time. Once again, the issue can be well framed in terms of "the vague." The text is never finished; closure is always deferred. The text for James is doomed to eternal incompleteness, first, in the sense that any theory, as directional, is incomplete; second, the text as such is vague in the sense that it is James's own form of rebellion, of living "heroically," as it were. This is one reason why *Some Problems of Philosophy* stops, or does not stop, in the middle of an arch. Ironically, any "direct" encounter with reality that religion meets "head on" becomes more and more of a problem for James, and it does so *through language, through theory, through the text*. He may have "wanted to be healthy" in spite of his sympathy for "sick souls," as Bjork suggests,[34] but his theories about the fragile human self and about reality in a quasi-Derridian sense both "describe" and "defer" (i.e., put off) their respective objects.[35] But the outlook is more optimistic than that of Derrida. "Possibilities exist," as James would say. The "texts" are, in the last, or nonlast analysis, "vague," like the items with which they deal. The texts problematize or cast doubt on direct encounters, but they also hold open some possibility for such an encounter if the text is taken as *directional* rather than descriptive. I return to this in the Conclusion.

Charlene Haddock Seigfried sees three crises in James's writings: the first, the well-known 1867–70 encounter with nihilism; the second, occurring around 1895, as James began more and more to realize that the descriptive positivism of the *Principles* was inadequate; and the third, which I concentrate on here, as occurring explicitly in the fifth chapter of *A Pluralistic Universe*. For Seigfried, it is in this fifth chapter of *A Pluralistic Universe*, one of direct personal confession, that James renounces the ability of "intellectualist logic" to deal with reality. She astutely points out that "the third crisis . . . is misleading if understood as revealing a shift to a different basis of explanation not already present in the early and middle writings." [36] Any such sequencing of James as going, say, from psychology to philosophy in whole cloth is certainly problematic. But there is something to be said, as the crises proliferate, for the thesis that James's whole life was a crisis of one sort or another, that he constantly strove to live life intensely and zestfully, though not always with equal success. Seigfried goes on to view James as rejecting only "classical foundationalism," and this only at the end of his philosophical career; and she interprets James as offering in place of classical foundationalism a "thoroughly pragmatic, post-modern rationalism." [37] While this is a very insightful view of James, it does seem to *tame* the vague a bit too much—or at least not to highlight the importance of the "inarticulate" dimension of his thought. One way to bring this out is to note that the textual-autobiographical locus of the third crisis, that is, *A Pluralistic Universe*, ends with explicit reference to the implicit, or to "the faith ladder." Even at the very end of his life, then, James was acting as he did in the beginning, in the 1867–70 crisis; but his style of rebellion had now changed, as had its scope. One can look at 1868–70 as the time of James's first and perhaps major *existential* crisis; and at 1896 (i.e., the publication date of "The Will to Believe") as the textual verbalization and legitimization of that type of response. Here the *style* of rebellion has changed somewhat, from existential to textual. The *scope* of "The Will to Believe" is still in question, however, since James sometimes talks as if it applies only in specific areas, like religion and morals, and sometimes speaks as if it is the criteria—namely, "forced," "living," and "momentous" options—that are the determining characteristics. It makes a great deal of difference whether one sees the vague as applying only to selected domains or whether one asserts that reality as such is vague, at least in the sense that it overflows our logical and linguistic structures.

A Pluralistic Universe, though ostensively concerned with a religious theme, contains some of James's most radical metaphysical statements. These statements explicitly point beyond themselves, that is, they highlight the inarticulate and the vague. James's own metaphysics is not neutral on the religious question, but what he also realizes somewhat more clearly here than, say, in "The Will to Believe" is that *no* metaphysics—scientific, positivistic, or otherwise—is neutral. This second position was always available in the Jamesian corpus, but it was inadequately developed. As early as "The Sentiment of Rationality" (1879, 1882) James tells us that the "bottom of being is left logically opaque to us,"[38] and applauds our "ontological wonder-sickness."[39] But the more radical dimension of James's thought is somewhat hidden by some of his quasi-positivistic descriptions in *The Principles*,[40] by his interest in preserving a viable place for religious experience, and by his concern not to have this experience replaced by linguistic theory. The ultimate outcome, however, though put off for a while, is a radical one. A reconstructed view of James's position shows that he not only viewed the area of religion as vague, and hence in some sense not easily accessible, but that in such traditional areas as perception, science, language, and metaphysics he developed outlooks that are best framed or articulated in terms of the importance of the vague.

Gerald Myers has astutely stated that "all great thinkers, including James, make interpreters of their readers."[41] The present work is no exception to this observation; it makes no claim for either completeness or impartiality, but rather proceeds from the perspectival stance that James himself espoused. The first part, "Interpretations," shows how James's religious concerns move him toward an overall metaphysical position—one of "reality as vague." The second part, "Conversations," takes its cue from James's texts as "vague in the sense of being unfinished," and attempts to carry on a dialogue with other philosophers, or with their texts. Finally, the third part, "Applications," also commences from the directional nature of James's text, in that it attempts to put those texts to work in concrete situations.

PART ONE

INTERPRETATIONS

A great resource of America was vagueness. American uncertainties, products of ignorance and progress, were producers of optimism and energy. Although few acknowledged it, in the era between the Revolution and the Civil War this vagueness was a source of American strength. . . . The nation would long profit from having been born without ever having been conceived.
DANIEL J. BOORSTIN, The Americans: The National Experience

What is crucial . . . , from the philosophical side, is that the press of environment as a decisive formulator of thought about the basic structures of the world became the outstanding characteristic of the American temperament. Pragmatism, so often regarded as the typically American philosophical product, is but a pale reflection of an ingrained attitude affirming the supremacy of experience over thought. It should be emphasized that this sense of the ineptness of anticipatory and defining concepts for managing experience was not only paramount in the early colonial period but was characteristic of the growth of American culture until the end of the nineteenth century.
JOHN J. MCDERMOTT, "The American Angle of Vision"

Chapter One

"The Vague" in *The Principles* and "the More" in *The Varieties*: Some Preliminaries

As early as James's first book-length work, *The Principles of Psychology* (1890), it is evident that the theme of vagueness, so important in his personal confrontation with death, has become a major element of his view of the fragile human self. In this chapter we argue that James's "stream of consciousness" is actually a plea that the quest for certainty and objectivity be rejected, and that life be lived as "richly" and "intensely" as possible. Once James worked out the importance of "the vague" in *The Principles*, he never abandoned it, though he sometimes underestimated its range of applicability. One area, among many, where he found a sense of the vague to be important was the religious dimension of life. James suggests that religious experience is both "rich" and "intense" precisely insofar as it is vague or ambiguous. Let us first draw out the significance of these terms.

The words "extension," [1] "profusion," [2] "continuously changing," [3] "overflows," [4] "manyness in oneness," [5] "experience . . . can grow," [6] "fringed by a 'more,'" [7] "concatenated," [8] and so on are used interchangeably by James to emphasize the richness of experience. Basically, we have failed to notice the profuseness of life in three ways.

First of all, we have assumed that experience is finished,

whereas it is actually still "in the making." As unfinished, experience is both a process and a product. Initially, James's intention was to show that this was the case for consciousness, but the position taken in *The Principles* eventually led him to the view that experience in general was unfinished. This view is not available in terms of a static subject/object dichotomy.

Second, we have assumed that experience is made up of substantive parts, that these have a value, and that the transitive parts are simply neutral connectives. Again, starting from the view that consciousness, as an unfinished stream, had interpenetrating substantive and transitive parts, James ultimately wound up asserting an identical view of experience.

Third, we have relied too heavily on language and on concepts qua concepts, which are themselves oriented toward exclusivity rather than integrated richness. If experience is unfinished or open-ended, it is incapable of complete conceptualization, much less of linguistic systematizing. At its basic level, life does not reveal itself to the exclusivity of the subject/object dichotomy. Bewitched by language, we are prone to presume that if there is no word for an experience, such an experience does not exist.

James was continually concerned with the unacknowledged richness of life, and his refusal to accept a system at the cost of richness gives us a clue as to the type of "hypothesis" he would uphold. For James, that characterization or attitude toward life will be most significant which is most inclusive, which incorporates most completely the richness encountered in experience.

But richness by itself is not enough. The very fact that life was richer than the subject/object dichotomy renders experience intense. If the categories "subjective" and "objective" cannot be employed as exclusive, it follows that people are always going to find themselves involved *in* experience. As a result, life is necessarily intense.

The words "zest," [9] "selection," [10] "chooses," [11] "interest," [12] "decided," [13] "will," [14] "risk," [15] "intensity," [16] and so forth are used by James to show that we are participators *in* life rather than spectators *at* the game of life. According to Ellen Suckiel, "it is difficult to find one single term to refer to these goals, desires, purposes, ideals, preferences, wants, and needs" in James.[17] (She selects "interests" as an overall term; I have selected "intensity.") Life represents itself as a challenge to which we must respond. To decide not to decide is in itself to make a decision. In this sense, we are all artists carving out experience. The world is "really malleable, waiting to receive its final touches at our hands."[18]

Moment-to-moment living, however, or intensity for the sake of intensity, was not James's goal. Intensity was partly cumulative or progressive, not just instantaneous or atomistic. Indeed, to interpret the intensity of life as a group of sequential uninvolved "droplets" would be to commit "vicious intellectualism." Rather must intensity be viewed as inherently connected with richness. Indeed, they are two sides of the same coin.

Vagueness in *The Principles of Psychology*

The Principles of Psychology, the first major work of James, was twelve years in the making and earned for him the title "father of American psychology." Here I confine myself primarily to an analysis of the "stream of consciousness," negatively, in its (implicit) rejection of the subject/object dichotomy, and positively, in terms of richness and intensity as the new criteria James adopts.[19]

James himself divides the characteristics of consciousness into five. The fact that he used only four characteristics when writing the shorter version of *The Principles*[20] would seem to indicate that these divisions were overlapping rather than mutually exclusive. One way of grouping the divisions of the stream might be to say that the first, fourth, and fifth characteristics emphasize intensity, while the second and third remind us that intensity is cumulative, or that richness is a cocriterion. It is this division that I shall adopt here. According to James:

1) Every thought tends to be part of a personal consciousness;

4) It [consciousness] always appears to deal with objects independent of itself; [that is, it is cognitive, or possesses the function of knowing];

5) It is interested in some parts of these objects to the exclusion of others, and welcomes or rejects—*chooses* from among them . . . —all the while.[21]

In calling all thoughts "personal," James immediately stresses involvement on the part of each of us. There are no impartial thoughts existing as transcendental spectators, impartially viewing the game of life. Every thought is "owned," or better, "tends to appear" as owned, thus allowing for the "facts of sub-conscious personality" or "*secondary personal selves.*"[22] James is here advocating the efficacy of consciousness. The reason is simple: consciousness must have a part to play if life is to be intense. Consciousness must be personally involved if we are to get from life that sense of zest for which James was always looking. At this stage, however, the only way James sees to uphold the active power of consciousness is to adopt a dualism. Indeed, there are several places in *The Principles* where he explicitly adopts a dualistic approach. For example: "*The psychologist's attitude toward cognition . . . is a thoroughgoing dualism.* It supposes two elements, mind knowing and thing known, and treats them as irreducible. Neither gets out of itself or into the other, neither in any way *is* the other, neither *makes* the other."[23] The problem confronting James is clear: what approach to life will allow for the personal efficacy of consciousness, and hence the intensity of experience? A dualistic approach would satisfy this demand, but at the cost of bifurcating experience. By separating experience into two parts, dualism impoverishes the original richness of experience. While James himself is unclear here, and continually rejects and then returns to dualism in *The Principles*, there are at least some indications of the discomfort he felt in adopting dualism. This is most readily seen in the analysis of the fourth and fifth characteristics of consciousness.

Consciousness, as cognitive, appears to deal with, or "intends," an object. Conception is defined by James as "neither the mental state nor what the mental state signifies, but the relation between the two, namely, the *function* of the mental state in signifying just that particular thing."[24] Consciousness as portrayed here is dipolar. A division of experience into consciousness on one side and objectivity on the other is an inadequate abstraction. A richer view of consciousness than the one posited by dualism is needed. James realized that in talking about experience we may say either atoms-producing-consciousness or consciousness-produced-by-atoms. To say either atoms alone or consciousness alone precisely equally mutilates the truth.[25] James here is looking for a view of consciousness that will, at one and the same time, keep it as active and keep it as continuous with the rest of experience. His initial step is to assert that a distinction must be made between the object-of-consciousness and the object-in-itself. Consciousness, as intention, is constitutive of the former of these. Furthermore, since consciousness is intentional at all times, the only object I am aware of in being conscious is the constituted-object. Widespread failure on the part of psychologists to note the inadequacy of the division of experience into the categories "subjective" and "objective" has led to what James called the "psychologist's fallacy:"

> The great snare of the psychologist is the *confusion of his own standpoint with that of the mental fact* about which he is making his report. . . . The psychologist . . . stands outside the mental state he speaks of. Both itself and its object are objects for him. Now when it is a *cognitive* state (percept, thought, concept, etc.) he ordinarily has no other way of naming it than as the thought, percept,

etc., *of that object.* He himself, meanwhile, knowing the
self-same object in *his* way, gets easily led to suppose that
the thought, which is *of* it, knows it in the same way in
which he knows it, although this is often very far from
being the case.[26]

Though James himself is not as clear here as he could be, nonetheless he seems to be moving toward the position that each thought,
including the psychologist's thought, is constitutive of an object,
and therefore no analysis of consciousness as dualistically divided
into subjective and objective is correct. Hence any awareness of
reality can no longer be regarded as impartial, because each and
every awareness of experience is intentional, that is, constitutive.
If this is so, all conscious experience would seem to be intense
because we are forced to mold and shape, or "create," our objects.
In all conscious experience we would be artists, selecting certain
aspects to highlight and neglecting others. This point needs to be
emphasized, because its implications extend far beyond *The Principles.* From a metatheoretical or self-reflective perspective, *The
Principles* needs to be viewed as an interpretive text and not just
as a descriptive one.[27]

It is the fifth characteristic of consciousness that emphasizes
its being interested more in one part of its object than another, and
its welcoming and rejecting, or choosing all the while it thinks.
The senses are nothing but selective organs, which pick out, from
among all the movements of experience, those that fall within
certain limits of velocity. The barest perception possible is focalization. We see *this* as opposed to *that, here* as opposed to *there,*
and so on. "Out of what is in itself an undistinguishable, swarm-
ing *continuum,* devoid of distinction or emphasis, our senses make
for us, by attending to this motion and ignoring that, a world
full of contrasts, or sharp accents, of abrupt changes, of pictur-
esque light and shade."[28] Two insights can be gleaned here. First
of all, James is again emphasizing the active role of consciousness. Life is intense because by our choices we are creating it.

So-called things, from this point of view, are not separate impartial entities, but rather "special groups of sensible qualities, which happen practically or aesthetically to interest us, to which we therefore give substantive names, and which we exalt to [the] . . . exclusive status of independence and dignity."[29] Nevertheless, it is only because the simplest sensation is richer than we have heretofore acknowledged that selection is possible. What we hear is not simply thunder, but rather thunder-preceded-by-silence.[30] I shall return to this when discussing the second and third characteristics. For the present, let us note simply that selectivity makes consciousness intense, but one must select *from* something. It is only because the present moment of consciousness is ongoing, has *more* to it than we have noticed, that selection can take place. Focalization, in brief, depends on a fringe. This fringe is the unfinished continuum, in which we find ourselves by our selective choices.

Not only do sensations select (e.g., a given velocity of sound waves to "hear"), but also from the sensations we do have, we select some to call "true" and some to call "false." Thus, for example, I select the view of my table top as square and to be the "true" one, relegating other possibilities, such as two acute and two obtuse angles, to the status of "perspectival."[31] In two senses, then, perception is selective. Reasoning proper is even more selective, consisting as it does in a choice of one aspect of an object as the "essence" and a subsuming of the object, now properly labeled, into its proper conceptual framework. Logically speaking, there are many such frameworks, and we simply select the one that is most suitable to our present needs. Consciousness, then, is selective at all levels. "Consciousness is at all times primarily a *selecting agency*. Whether we take it in the lowest sphere of sense, or in the highest of intellection, we find it always doing one thing, choosing one out of several of the materials so presented to its notice, emphasizing and accentuating that and suppressing as far as possible all the rest. The item emphasized is always in close connection with some *interest* felt by consciousness to be paramount at the time." [32] We are always aware, then, in terms of our needs and interests. To be conscious at all is to be partial, or in other terms, rationality is prescriptive. Life is intense because each of us is involved with its making. There is no possibility of being impartial or of arriving at objectivity. Jacques Barzun realized the connection between ambiguity and creativity in art, as the following quotation indicates: "[In *The Principles*] James struck a death blow at Realism. The then prevailing views of the mind were that it copied reality like a photographic plate, that it received and assembled the elements of experience like a machine, that it combined ideas like a chemist. For this 'scientist' mind, James substituted one that was a born artist—a wayward, creative mind, impelled by inner wants, fringed with mystery, and capable of infinitely subtle, unrecordable nuances." [33]

But this is only half of the story. A cursory reading of James's statements on selectivity might lead one to conclude that one can select capriciously anything one wants to be aware of and, further, that each of these selections has no relation to others. This is by no means the case. Selection is possible only because consciousness is an unfinished stream, from which I am *continually* forced to choose. The choosing renders life intense, but each choosing, precisely because it is a moment in a cumulative process, cuts off alternatives for the future. In brief, James's defense of the efficacy of consciousness is part and parcel of his view that consciousness is richer than we have realized, that it has substantive and transitive parts, which overlap. These are discussed under the second and third characteristics of consciousness, namely, that:

   2) Within each personal consciousness thought is always changing, [and]

   3) Within each personal consciousness thought is sensibly continuous. [34]

The first of these two aspects asserts that change is a definite element in consciousness and must be dealt with as such. No single state of consciousness, once it has gone, can recur and be identical with what it was before. Something has occurred in between these two appearances; these interim occurrences cannot be ignored, save by arbitrary whim. At the very least, the time of the two appearances is different. Furthermore, the second of the two must take the first one into account, in terms of the present context. Each present state of consciousness, then, is partly determined by the nature of the entire past succession. As James says, "Experience is remoulding us every moment, and our mental reaction on every given thing is really a resultant of our experience of the whole world up to that date."[35] Here James clearly casts his vote with the reality of change. Each and every moment of consciousness is at least temporally different from any previous one. As temporally different it must take into account different circumstances. Each succeeding present moment has one additional past moment to take into account and therefore cannot be taken as identical with it. What has happened, however, is that certain schools of thought, intrigued with finding factual certainty "beneath" this "apparent" process, have reduced this rich complexity to simplicity. Seizing on one aspect of an experience as basic and finding this aspect repeated in other experiences, these schools have "taken the part for the whole," ignored the temporal context of each moment of consciousness, and articulated a view of consciousness wherein all its variations are reduced to combinations of certain simple, basic elements. The second aspect of consciousness emphasizes the fact that experience is richer than we have admitted. It has contextual nuances that must be taken into account; in particular, the temporal aspect of each moment of consciousness cannot be ignored. Change is real; no thought can be had twice in the exact same manner. As James himself so forcefully puts it, "*A permanently existing 'idea' or 'Vorstellung' which makes its appearance before the footlights of consciousness at periodical intervals, is as mythological an entity as the Jack of Spades.*"[36]

Not only does consciousness change, but the changing is an ongoing process. As an unfinished continuum, consciousness has both substantive and transitive parts. The transitions between two substantive moments of consciousness are as real as the substantive moments themselves. Conscious states, in other words, are continuous, because they are connected by transitional fringes. For example, James asks that we consider what a conscious awareness of thunder would be like: "Into the awareness of the thunder itself the awareness of the previous silence creeps and continues; for what we hear when the thunder crashes is not thunder *pure*, but thunder-breaking-upon-silence-and-contrasting-with-it."[37]

These transitive elements are represented in language by such words as "of," "and," "but," and so forth. These are all contrast words. We are aware of this *and not* that, this part *of* that, and so on. Once again, we are reminded that consciousness, as selective, is forced to mold experience. The experience in and through which the molding takes place presents itself as a continuum, or in James's words, a stream: "Consciousness . . . does not appear to itself chopped up in bits. Such words as 'chain' or 'train' do not describe it fitly as it presents itself in the first instance. It is nothing jointed; it flows. A 'river' or a 'stream' are the metaphors by which it is most naturally described."[38]

In each conscious experience, then, there is always a main substantive point, arrived at in accordance with our needs at the time and surrounded by a periphery of transitional aspects, that is, that this point chosen as substantive is *not* that, is *part* of this larger whole, is *like* that in one respect but not in another respect, and so forth. The point here is that each and every moment of consciousness is contextually articulated in terms of transitive elements and that these elements are part and parcel of conscious awareness. These transitive parts are relations; they are as real for James as the substantive parts that they relate: "If there be such things as feelings at all, *then so surely as relations between objects exist in rerum naturâ, so surely, and more surely, do feelings exist to which these relations are known.*"[39] Conscious experience is richer than we have realized. It is so because it contains not only substantive elements, represented by nouns and adjectives, but also transitive elements, represented by disjunctions and conjunctions. These latter are both as real for conscious awareness as the substantive parts that they connect. They are found among the objects of the stream, which *is* a stream because it is composed, in a nonreductive manner, of interpenetrating substantive and transitive parts. Note that *both* the disjunctive and conjunctive transitions are real. A decision to recognize the ontological status of substantive parts and disjunctive parts would lead to the atomism of traditional empiricism. But a decision to recognize the validity of substantive parts and the conjunctive transitions would tend to reject pluralism and, ultimately, to dismiss change as an illusion. James sees no reason for rejecting either transitive part. The result is a view of consciousness as a stream partially conjunctive and partially disjunctive.

Putting the second and third aspects together, then, we get a view of consciousness as a continuum, made up of substantive and transitive parts, and yet changing because involved in a temporal process. Every image in conscious experience is "steeped and dyed in the free water that flows round it. With it goes the sense of its relations, near and remote, the dying echo of whence it came to us, the dawning sense of whither it is to lead. . . . If I recite *a, b, c, d, e, f, g,* at the moment of my uttering *d,* neither *a, b, c,* nor *e, f, g,* are out of my consciousness altogether, but both, after their respective fashions, 'mix their dim lights' with the stronger one of the *d.*"[40]

Taken together, then, these two aspects of consciousness present us with a picture, in "broad strokes," of an ongoing, unfinished continuum; within this process certain aspects are focalized on and others remain on the fringe, or periphery, of consciousness. The most basic element of experience has duration here; it is a movement-going-into-the-past-and-a-new-tendency-toward-the-future. Each moment has a rearward- and forward-looking end. The present is no pinpoint or knife edge; rather, it should be viewed as a saddle back,[41] having a breadth of its own. As Gerald Myers has noted: "It was important, James believed, to realize that vagueness often characterizes our feelings and sensations; introspective psychology, to be accurate, must acknowledge this vagueness, and at the level of sensation and feeling—the 'guts' of experience—vagueness is usually the harbinger of something further to be detected, the promise of a potential discovery."[42] Here, for example, is James's analysis of a sensation:

> A simple sensation . . . is an abstraction, and all our concrete states of mind are representations of objects with some amount of complexity. Part of the complexity is the echo of the objects just past, and, in a less degree, perhaps, the foretaste of those just to arrive. Objects fade out of consciousness slowly. If the present thought is of A B C D E F G, the next one will be of B C D E F G H, and the one after that of C D E F G H I—the lingerings of the past dropping successively away, and the incomings of the future making up the loss. These lingerings of old objects, these incomings of new, are the germs of memory and expectation, the retrospective and prospective sense of time. They give that continuity to consciousness without which it could not be called a stream.[43]

Consciousness, in brief, is much richer than we have realized. It has much more than substantive parts, existing atomistically and awaiting the unifying idea of an outside agent. Rather are the relating transitions in consciousness to be taken into account; these are of both a disjunctive and conjunctive nature. Furthermore, consciousness is temporal, and the situational aspect of all thoughts, the fact that we can never have the same thought twice, can no longer be ignored. Note here that it is precisely because consciousness is an ongoing continuum, in which a simple sensation is impossible, that we have to be selective. Since the sensible present has duration and is characterized in terms of a coming-to-be-and-a-passing-away, we are always focusing on one part of it. On the one hand, conscious experience is intense because we are forced to make decisions, to choose, to intend. But the selecting is a cumulative process. On the other hand, consciousness is far richer than we have noticed; it is unfinished and has interpenetrant substantive and transitive parts. As such it causes us to be selective. In a word, the richness of consciousness demands its intensity, and vice versa. James himself found it difficult to articulate both of these notions with a single word. His closest attempt comes in the stream-of-consciousness chapter, where he says: "It is, in short, the re-instatement of the vague to its proper place in our mental life which I am anxious to press on the attention."[44] Conscious experience is vague, in the sense of being richer than any formula. It is unfinished, and here could also be called vague. Finally, it is as vague that consciousness demands selectivity. In brief, experience, as an unfinished continuum, demands an intense life on the part of each of us, and experience is infinitely rich in the sense of being still in the making, since the last person in experience has not had his or her say. The net result is the attempt to maintain as much of the richness at as intense a level as possible. James himself at this stage, however, does not indicate clearly how his own outlook, from a hermeneutical perspective, applies also to itself. This does become clearer in later texts, especially in *A Pluralistic Universe*. But before turning to this, let us look at James's first order or descriptive account of religious experience.

The Religious Experience as Vague

One area, among many, where the importance of the vague is apparent is that of religion. In *The Varieties of Religious Experience*, James specifically rejects rationalistic a priori systems; he opts instead for a view of religion that sees the human person as becoming coterminous with a vague "more" existing on the periphery of consciousness. Myers has noted that James "saw religion as a vague response to a vague human need."[45] He points out the specific connection James saw here. "Psychologists and religious mystics alike understand that any experience, when we reflect upon it, has no definite boundary but radiates from its center into a surrounding *more*. (The word *more* was a favorite of James's, for it expressed his belief that we should never cease our moral striving.)" [46]

The very title, that is, *The VARIETIES of Religious Experience*, gives us a clue to James's intent. The book itself is one long plea that religious experience is pervasive. Taking his examples from all areas of organized religion, James again and again ostensively makes this point—there is simply no ignoring the amount of "evidence" for religious experience. For the same reason, the pervasiveness of religion, no finished formula is available. "The word 'religion' cannot stand for any single principle or essence, but is rather a collective name." [47] This plea for the richness of religious experience is negatively expressed in James's harsh critiques against vicious intellectualism in religion: "The intellectualism in religion which I wish to discredit . . . assumes to construct religious objects out of the resources of logical reason alone. . . . It reaches [its conclusions] in an a priori way." [48] And again, "In all sad sincerity I think we must conclude that the attempt to demonstrate by purely intellectual processes the truth of the deliverances of direct religious experience is absolutely hopeless." [49]

There was, in James's opinion, no one formula that could contain the whole of religious experience. Any such dogmatic statement would have been diametrically opposed to his unfinished universe. Nevertheless, James, at least in the final chapters of this work, does attempt some sort of justification as to why one should opt for religious experience. I believe that the justification is made in terms of richness and intensity, and I confine my present analysis of *The Varieties* to these two aspects.

The pervasiveness of religious experience is indicated early in *The Varieties*, as is seen in the following attempt to define religion: "Religion, whatever it is, is a man's total reaction upon life, so why not say that any total reaction upon life is a religion?" [50]

Here we can see clearly the "extensity" of religious experience. I must react, for the same reason I am forced to make moral decisions—there is no possibility of being neutral. A total reaction, for James, would be "religious." And the criteria used to measure total reactions are richness and intensity. Let us first look at the richness of the religious life.

Acting as a psychologist interested in the religious experience of a person rather than in any organized religion, James continually connects this religious experience with the subliminal area of consciousness:

> We cannot, I think, avoid the conclusion that in religion we have a department of human nature with unusually close relations to the transmarginal or subliminal region . . . [that the subliminal region] . . . is obviously the larger part of each of us, for it is the abode of everything that is latent and the reservoir of everything that passes unrecorded or unobserved. . . . [E]xperiences making their entrance through . . . [this] door have had emphatic influence in shaping religious history.[51]

We are reminded here of the development of the stream of consciousness in terms of an ongoing focus-fringe continuum, and also of James's metaphysical position that experience always comes to us "fringed by a more." His interest in religion is partially based on the fact that the religious person is constantly striving to acknowledge this peripheral aspect of his or her consciousness. In religion a person becomes conscious that this *"higher part is coterminous and continuous with a* MORE *of the same quality, which is operative in the universe outside of him, and which he can keep in working touch with, and in a fashion get on board of and save himself when all his lower being has gone to pieces in the wreck."*[52] For religious persons, the sensible world is only part of a more spiritual one, with which they are continually trying to achieve harmony. It is this quest for a more enriched experience in religion, this attempt to get at the subliminal region of consciousness, that James found so enticing. In *The Principles*, James continually argued against the "vicious intellectualism"[53] that dismissed certain aspects of consciousness. This attempt to take into account the subliminal regions of consciousness was paramount in James, and he found religious experience dealing with those very aspects. While it is true that origin in the subliminal region "is no infallible credential" and that whatever experience does originate there must "run the gauntlet of confrontation with the total context of experience,"[54] it is nonetheless the case that a religious attitude does deal with the richness of experience. "Weight, movement, velocity, direction, position, what thin, pallid, uninteresting ideas! How could the richer animistic aspects of Nature, the peculiarities and oddities that make phenomena picturesquely striking or expressive, fail to have been first singled out and followed by philosophy as the more promising avenue to the knowledge of Nature's life? Well, it is still in these richer animistic and dramatic aspects that religion delights to dwell."[55]

In brief, one reason why James finds religious experience so worthwhile is that it consistently remains open to the richness of experience. As a psychologist he expressed this in terms of a religious consciousness dealing with the subliminal. Consciousness is fringed by a more; religion deals with that "more." As a result, religious experience enables one to build a richer experience. "Among the buildings-out of religion which the mind spontaneously indulges in, the aesthetic motive must never be forgotten. . . . Although some persons aim most at intellectual purity and simplification, for others, *richness* is the supreme imaginative requirement."[56] The variety of James's demonstrations and his emphasis on vagueness leave no doubt as to which of the two options (i.e., animated vs. nonanimated nature) he would align himself with. Religious experience is enriching; it is forever in quest of the "more," the "ever not quite" of experience.

But this again is only half the story. Not only is richness to be found in religious experience, but intensity also. Elsewhere, James states that the "universe is no longer a mere *It* to us, but a *Thou*, if we are religious." [57] A human being, in responding to the presence of a Thou, lives life intensely. The emotion encountered in a religious experience "overcomes temperamental melancholy and imparts endurance to the Subject, or a zest, or a meaning, or an enchantment and glory to the common objects of life." [58]

Precisely because the religious experience deals with the marginal, the fringe, the more, and so forth, it is demanding. Religious persons, whose reactions to life are "total," are necessarily taking a chance. They are "betting on" the ideal impulses that come from their subliminal region. They are willing to chance giving up a present moment for a vaguely held ideal. "A man's conscious wit and will, so far as they strain towards the ideal, are aiming at something only dimly and inaccurately imagined." [59] Again we notice that the concept of "vagueness"—so useful in describing the richness of religious experience in terms of the subliminal— also serves to denote the necessity of taking a chance. Religion for James includes "a new zest, which adds itself like a gift to life." [60] Again in describing a religious virtue like charity, we find the notion of risk at the very center of its possible realization: "If things are ever to move upward, some one must be ready to take the first step, and assume the risk of it. No one who is not willing to try charity, to try non-resistance as the saint who is always willing, can tell whether these methods will or will not succeed." [61]

The importance of risk, zest, intensity as a common element in all truly religious experiences constitutes the second reason why James opted for rather than against it. Religious experience is risk-filled; here it is that one can reach the heights of satisfaction or fall to the depths of despair. "Here if anywhere," James says, "is the genuinely strenuous life." [62] Once again, James is acting as a psychologist here, and the basis of his thought is to be found in *The Principles*. There we found a view of consciousness as selective, and an articulation of self-realization in terms of success-over-aspiration. [63] A stoic would simply reduce all tension, all risk, by reducing his aspirations to zero. For James, resignation was impossible; to decide not to decide was a decision. "It makes a tremendous emotional and practical difference to one whether one accept the universe in the drab discolored way of stoic resignation to necessity, or with the passionate happiness of Christian saints." [64] Growth, James realized, is dependent on tension and risk; if one is to strive for the growth of experience, for a richer life, one must take chances, one must live intensely. "No fact in human nature is more characteristic than its willingness to live on a chance. The existence of the chance makes the difference, as Edmund Gurney says, between a life of which the keynote is resignation and a life of which the keynote is hope." [65]

In brief, at a preliminary level *The Varieties of Religious Experience* makes three very significant points:

1. In approaching religious experience psychologically, it reminds us that James's criteria here will be the same as in *The Principles of Psychology*: richness and intensity.

2. In terms of richness, religious experience is valuable because it is continually open, groping for a richer, more integrated experience.

3. In terms of intensity, religious experience continually demands involvement, zest, chance on the part of each of us.

This emphasis on vagueness, richness, and intensity is mainly of a descriptive nature in *The Principles*, and the emphasis tends to focus on a descriptive account of the personal in *The Varieties*. But his position here is not as neutral as it might seem, and James became more and more aware of his presuppositions as he turned toward metaphysics. In the following chapter I begin my investigation of this process of awareness.

Chapter Two

Vagueness, God, and Actual Possibility

Pragmatism

We are by now familiar with two predominant criticisms of William James. One of these has it that James was at bottom an empiricist—advocating an outlook that is positivistic and nominalist in character. Proponents of this view point to James's emphasis on the importance of the "cash value" of terms, his disbelief in systems of rationalism, and his rejection of an all-powerful, all-seeing God.

Another interpretation of James, which appears to be the opposite of this one in some ways, has it that James is really subjectivistic through and through, that his philosophical outlook rests on a sheer relativism. Proponents of this view emphasize the importance of emotive feelings, or sentiments, for James, the right of each person to opt for a particular belief, the thesis that belief in a fact can help bring about fact, and James's emphasis on the personal as opposed to the communal. Indeed, some people accuse James of holding both of these seemingly contradictory positions simultaneously. In sum, as Eugene Fontinell has put it, "there is a well-recognized ambiguity in James's pragmatic method that allows for both a positivistic and a personalistic reading."[1]

Critics of these two positions have asserted the impossibility of making any sense out of life without reference to the reality of generals or universals. As long as reality is taken to be the atomic individual—whether in a nominalistic or a personalistic sense— no overall picture of the universe is possible. This is so because in such a system all generalizations are, as such, mere empty concepts. They deal only with abstract possibility, not with reality. Critics of the empiricist and personal dimensions in James point out that in his outlook all statements about universals, or about future tendencies, deal only with the *possible* possibility—about the logical probabilities of something that might happen. Now without a doubt, the empirical and personal constitute seminal aspects of James's outlook. Indeed, I return to the personal dimension at the end of this section. But by itself, neither the personal nor the empirical is self-supporting.

The problem with such an atomistic approach has often been pointed out. To take one specific instance, given such a "particularist" position, no scientific laws are possible. Laws remain only compendia of individual events; they have no power of their own. Any statement concerning what *would* happen if such and such were to be done, that is, a contrary-to-fact conditional, is an attempt to deal with "actual possibility" as opposed to "possible possibility." Royce claimed that, without actual possibility, no adequate view of the universe is attainable; Peirce struggled long and hard with this issue, renouncing his early nominalism for a realism. But if one of his foremost interpreters, Arthur Burks, is right, Peirce's realism is incompatible with his pragmatism. The latter outlook allows for no pragmatic difference between "possible possibility" and "actual possibility," between statements like "If this is water, it will boil at 212°" and "If this were water, it would boil at 212°." In terms of "conceivable possible effects," nominalism and realism mean the same thing.[2]

There remains William James. Usually, he is interpreted as a philosopher who simply did not notice the difficulty here. On the face of it, this might seem true, but it does seem strange that, with all the uproar around him over the issue, it should remain completely unnoticed.

In this chapter another possible explanation is offered, namely, that James was at least *somewhat* aware of the problem of actual possibility versus possible possibility, and that he had resolved it—at least to his own satisfaction. This requires, first, a careful analysis of "God" as James presents this figure in *Pragmatism*. Ethics as a separate study never loomed large in Jamesian writings, perhaps because in his philosophy knowing has a moral dimension built in, in terms of choice. Religion, however, remains a pervasive influence in James, throughout almost all of his writings. He returns to the issue not only in *Pragmatism* but in *A Pluralistic Universe*, of course in *The Varieties of Religious Experience*, and, to a lesser degree, even in *Essays in Radical Empiricism*. Why? One tentative answer arises from *Pragmatism*; in that work God fulfills the role of the concrete universal, or actual possibility.

Recall, first of all, how important the God issue seems to be in *Pragmatism*. In the second chapter James reminds the reader that theological ideas, or mystical ones, can be pragmatically true, if they make a difference for concrete life. They must, however, "run the gauntlet of all . . . other beliefs."[3] In the third chapter he returns to the issue under the heading of "materialism versus theism" and "free will versus design," and again suggests that God can be pragmatically true.[4] By the end of the seventh lecture James is worried that pragmatism has been identified with "positivistic tough-mindedness."[5] So he spends the entire last chapter on God and religion—again urging that God can be pragmatically defined. Suckiel notes, correctly, that, "in his theory of pragmatic meaning . . . he [James] articulates quite a broad conception of what kinds of propositions are to count as having experiential implications. Thus, propositions concerning God's goodness, for example, are considered by James to be philosophically legitimate and important."[6]

In short, perhaps no other issue crops up so frequently throughout *Pragmatism*. Certainly no more unlikely candidate (considering James's empiricism) shows up there so often. I suggest that there must be a reason for this and that the God texts must be carefully analyzed.

⌐ To begin with, it is clear that James dismisses the God of rationalism as inadequate. That is, he rejects the rational answer that the world is *"ready-made and complete from all eternity"*[7]— kept in the mind of a preexistent, perfect, rational God. For our theme, the reason he explicitly rejects rationalism is quite important. James says: "Possibilities obtain in our world; in the absolute world, where all that is *not* is from eternity impossible, and all that *is* is necessary, the category of possibility has no application."[8] He reiterates his point: "The whole dilemma [over salvation] revolves pragmatically about the notion of the world's possibilities. . . . [T]he absolute makes all good things certain, and all bad things impossible (in the eternal, namely) and may be said to transmute the entire category of possibilities into categories more secure. . . . [T]he whole clash of rationalistic and empiricist religion is thus over the validity of possibility."[9] A rationalistic outlook, in short, did not allow for possibility—and for James, possibility was to be preserved at any cost.

But if rationalism cannot provide an adequate account of possibility and of God, can empiricism? To be sure, James favors many of the outlooks associated with empiricism, and particularly its pluralism. But it is quickly seen that empiricism too is incapable of the task. Traditional empiricism relies exclusively on the senses, and James here allows this as a necessary but not as a sufficient condition of establishing God. Consider, for example, James's statement that the one instance where the substance/accident distinction does make a difference, pragmatically speaking, is the Eucharist. Here the accidents (bread and wine) remain the same and the substance alters. "The substance-notion breaks into life, then, with tremendous effect, if once you allow that substances can separate from their accidents, and exchange these latter."[10] Even here James reminds the reader that a "pragmatic difference" is allowed *only* in conjunction with a much larger framework of previously accepted beliefs, that is, Christianity, some of these beliefs possessing sensible effects. I use this Eucharist example cautiously and do not wish to place more weight on it than it is worth. My point is only that "making a difference" is not simply defined by James as being found via one-to-one correspondence with external senses. A second instance of this point is James's clear refusal in chapter 5 of *Pragmatism* to set up any candidate as the final arbiter of pragmatic truth. "Common sense is *better* for one sphere of life, science for another, philosophic criticism for a third; but whether either be *truer* absolutely, Heaven only knows."[11] Third, an idea was pragmatically true for James not only if it dealt with present sensory experience but also if it remained loyal to the past. Prior experience, even though not currently available to the senses, plays a vital role in determining the pragmatic truth of an idea.[12]

In short, these examples make it quite clear that traditional empiricism is also an inadequate view. Going further, one reason traditional empiricism is inadequate is that it too does not allow for possibilities, as pragmatism does:

In the religious field . . . [pragmatism] is at a great advantage both over positivistic empiricism, with its antitheological bias, and over religious rationalism, with its exclusive interest in the remote, the noble, the simple, and the abstract in the way of conception.

In short, she widens the field of search for God. Rationalism sticks to logic and the empyrean. Empiricism sticks to the external senses. Pragmatism is willing to take anything, to follow either logic or the senses and to count the humblest and most personal experiences.[13]

Briefly, then, the God issue in James's *Pragmatism* is an extremely interesting one, because it furnishes some evidence that James did not intend to belong to either camp. Let us look at what James has to say of God in more detail.

In the last lecture of *Pragmatism*, James specifically takes up the question of religion and relates it to the idea of possibility. People who clash over the existence of God are fighting over this issue, so James applies the pragmatic test to the idea of possibility. An idea for James is true if it makes a difference, if it marries old truths to the novelty of the present situation, if it enables one to deal with the present moment while preserving as much of the past as possible. If a person calls something "possible," what difference does this make? "It makes at least this difference that if any one calls it impossible you can contradict him, if any one calls it actual you can contradict *him,* and if any one calls it necessary you can contradict him too." [14] James has here spelled out the *logical* meaning of the term "possible"; so far, the emphasis is on the cognitive dimension of the pragmatic method. So far, what has been said might well have been said by Peirce, or Royce, or several other philosophers, for that matter. But James is not satisfied with this definition (neither was Royce, ultimately). A merely logical definition is not sufficient, in James's opinion: "When you say a thing is possible, does that not make some farther difference in terms of actual fact?

It makes at least this negative difference that if the statement be true, it follows that *there is nothing extant capable of preventing* the possible thing. The absence of real grounds of interference may thus be said to make things *not impossible,* possible therefore in the *bare* or *abstract* sense." [15] Here James is struggling to attain something *more* than mere logical possibility. To be sure, an idea that is "pragmatically possible" must contain "no essential self-contradiction." Note that this is a necessary condition; the idea must be "meaningful." But it is not a sufficient condition. Just being *logically* possible is *insufficient* for an idea to be *pragmatically* possible. James here adds a factual state of affairs as part of the pragmatic notion of possibility, or more specifically, the nonexistence of a particular factual state of affairs, that is, those capable of preventing the occurrence of the possibility in question. Pragmatic possibility thus entails more than logical meaningfulness; it entails a factual situation.

Still James is dissatisfied. He has moved beyond logical possibility to a position whereby possibility entails negative existential situations, but he wants something more: "Most possibilities are not bare, they are concretely grounded, or well grounded, as we say. What does this mean pragmatically? It means not only that there are no preventive conditions present, but that some of the conditions of production of the possible thing actually are here."[16] If something is to be deemed pragmatically possible in the future, two states of affairs must *currently* exist in the present—one positive, one negative. If these two states of affairs do not exist in the present, then X is not *pragmatically* possible, even though it may remain logically possible.

Applying this to the issue of salvation, we have something like the following: Salvation as such is possible, which is to say it does not exist at the present moment. The world is such, however, that positive and negative factors exist regarding the possibility. If the positive ones were emphasized, salvation would become more probable. James puts it this way:

> Suppose that the world's author put the case to you before creation, saying: "I am going to make a world not certain to be saved, a world the perfection of which shall be conditional merely, the condition being that each several agent does its own 'level best.' I offer you the chance of taking part in such a world. Its safety, you see, is unwarranted. It is a real adventure, with real danger, yet it may win through. It is a social scheme of co-operative work genuinely to be done. Will you join the procession? Will you trust yourself and trust the other agents enough to face the risk?"[17]

Salvation here appears as a possibility, but it does so in a stronger sense than that of logical possibility. For our purpose, note that the issue of salvation can most easily be stated in terms of a contrary-to-fact conditional: if we were to do these things, salvation would exist. (Indicating we have not done them yet.)

Subjunctive conditionals present at least an apparent difficulty to an empiricist. R. B. Braithwaite explains the problem in the following manner:

> The problem which they [subjunctive conditionals] present to a Humean is the following dilemma. The constant-conjunction analysis leaves two choices open for the analysis of "If a thing is *A*, it is *B*." One choice is "Every *A* is *B*" taken, as traditional logic would say, "existentially," i.e., understood in such a way as to assert the existence of at least one thing which is *A*. The other alternative is "Every *A* is *B*" taken non-existentially, i.e., understood as not to assert the existence of an *A*.[18]

If we accept the first, "traditional" formulation, its logical equivalent is "Nothing is both *A* and non-*B*," together with the assertion "Something is *A*." The use of the subjunctive conditional here will add these assertions to the assertion that there is nothing which is *A*. This will result in self-contradiction.[19] If we accept the second formulation, its logical equivalent is merely the sole assertion "Nothing is both *A* and non-*B*." The use of the subjunctive conditional here would add the assertion that there is nothing which is *A*. It would then follow that, if nothing is *A*, nothing is both *A* and non-*B*. In this sense, the conjunction of the two assertions is logically equivalent to the first one taken by itself.[20] Thus we have at least an apparent dilemma: subjunctive conditionals are either self-contradictory or repetitive.

For our purposes, Braithwaite's answer to this dilemma is not important. It is inserted here merely to highlight the two alternatives open to an empiricist. I believe that James, acting as empiricist, did *not* reject the contrary-to-fact conditional but *did* reject that interpretation of it which viewed subjunctive conditionals as repetitive. In other words, James gave up logic as being completely capable of dealing with possibility. Had James maintained a strict Peircean emphasis on the cognitive dimension of pragmatism, his only alternative might well have been "possible (logical) possibility," as opposed to actual possibility.[21] (To be sure, Peirce can be interpreted more broadly, but some of his statements do lean toward an exclusively cognitive interpretation. I discuss this in Chapter Five, below.) For better or for worse, James changed the meaning of pragmatism to include more than the conceivable. Nowhere is this more evident than in the issue of God and salvation. For here James staunchly maintains actual possibility in terms of the contrary-to-fact conditional, and he rejects the side of Braithwaite's empiricist dilemma which views possibility as repetition. James chooses the self-contradictory, or in other words, his final interpretation of the salvation issue is one that transcends the formal boundaries of logic. James is extremely clear about this transgression: "In the end it is our faith and not our logic that decides such questions, and I deny the right of any pretended logic to veto my own faith. I find myself willing to take the universe to be really dangerous and adventurous, without therefore backing out and crying 'no play.' "[22]

Possibility, in short, was "existential" for James, and that term is meant to include more than the rational. A universe with possibility is not one capable of complete rational analysis. In a sense, it is the issue of God and salvation that gives radical possibility to the universe. Ultimately, the issue compels action:

> Does our act then *create* the world's salvation so far as it makes room for itself, so far as it leaps into the gap?
> . . . Here I take the bull by the horns, and in spite of the whole crew of rationalists and monists, of whatever brand they be, I ask, *why not?* Our acts, our turning-places, where we seem to ourselves to make ourselves and grow, are the parts of the world to which we are closest, the parts of which our knowledge is the most intimate and complete. Why should we not take them at their face-value?[23]

James then uses logic in *Pragmatism* to deal with God/salvation, but in doing so he demonstrates the inadequacy of logic to decide these issues. Logic remains necessary for James, but not sufficient. His purpose is rather to show that, after one has pushed reason as far as one can, there is still something left over that can only be "pointed at," or "acted on." Possibility remains actual for James, as opposed to merely possible, because it transcends logic: "Talk of logic and necessity and categories and the absolute and the contents of the whole philosophical machine-shop as you will, the only *real* reason I can think of why anything should ever come is that *some one wishes it to be here*. It is *demanded*—demanded, it may be, to give relief to no matter how small a fraction of the world's mass. This is *living reason*, and compared with it material causes and logical necessities are spectral things."[24] The idea of God, taken initially, is not self-contradictory. It has meaning. But that meaning is primarily cognitive and deals with logical possibility. The idea of God is developed in a more profound fashion as James attempts to allow for actual possibility. And James, faced with the choice between logical cohesiveness but repetition versus logical cohesiveness but a deeper level of "meaning," chose the latter option. In sum, as George Cotkin argues:

> The Jamesian pragmatic, activist world banished Hamlet. In his place were men and women actively engaged in a process of wresting salvation, both personal and collective, from the universe. James purposefully defined salvation in vague terms, not wanting theological or political disputes to interfere with his emphasis upon a strenuous morality. He only suggested that the process of salvation—that is, the reformation of the individual and the world—demanded that the individual add his or her "*fiat* to the *fiat* of the creator." Here James essentially repeated the argument of *The Will to Believe*.[25]

It is clear that the God issue remains a central one for the Jamesian corpus. A careful analysis of James's statements about God as found in *Pragmatism* reveals that the God issue preserves actual possibility for him. Actual possibility is not acceptable to traditional empiricism; rather does it appear as a repetitive or an irrational issue. James, for his part, uses logic to show the limitations of logic. To be sure, it allows for the importance of the empiricist approach. Indeed, for him, "making a difference" is an empirical matter. *But* "making a difference" is not strictly compatible with nor confirmable within the bounds of logic. More is involved. The God issue enables James to get to, or point toward, that "more." Here, as in so many other places in his writings, he was concerned with "the re-instatement of the vague to its proper place"[26] in our experience. ⸺

Nevertheless, while James finds fault with the empiricist model, he does not wind up in the camp of idealism. The Jamesian God is uncertain, finite, incomplete. As such, God is "irrational" from an idealist standpoint. But the God issue enables him to preserve actual possibility, as opposed to just logical possibility. In this sense James goes further than, or offers a different option than, Peirce. The latter's metaphysics and cosmology can be pragmatically defined only in terms of conceivable possible effects. As such, Peircean pragmatism has trouble allowing for the issue of actual possibility to arise. One way it might arise is if pragmatism as a theory of meaning were relegated to science and other ways found to deal with other areas of experience.[27] But the Jamesian view of pragmatism contains more than "conceivable possible effects"; it contains also the affective or the emotive. The God issue in James, when properly seen, is pragmatically definable and allows for actual possibility; but the pragmatism involved transcends the bounds of logic but not of experience. To the end, James remained an advocate of the thesis that the human being can experience *more* than he or she can intellectually conceptualize, and that this "more" is important, and fundamentally so.

While *Pragmatism* begins with an epistemology that quickly is seen to have underlying metaphysical presuppositions, in *A Pluralistic Universe*, James begins "from the other side," that is, the metaphysical. But here too it is quickly evident that James's metaphysics is also not neutral on the religious issue; and again the reason is the same: the preservation of actual possibility in a vague, uncertain universe.

A Pluralistic Universe

Some of James's most mature statements on metaphysics are to be found in *A Pluralistic Universe*. What is often ignored, however, is the crucial role faith plays in his final position. As I have noted, James is sometimes accused of being a nominalist, that is, of not condoning actual possibility. This is oftentimes verbalized in terms of a contrary-to-fact conditional in the subjunctive form and is said to require the reality of "generals" or universal ideas. It is well known that James had little tolerance for the block universe of essential archetypes. Acting as an empiricist, however, James confronted the issue of actual possibility and solved it from an empiricist point of view by advocating a realist position.

In this section I shall look at three topics: the setting of *A Pluralistic Universe*, the relationship of logic to reality, and the actual role philosophic systems themselves play in terms of the "faith ladder." The residual effect of these three issues is to demand a universe with actual possibility. James saw this and acted accordingly. Let us see how this comes about.

The Setting of A Pluralistic Universe

James had originally entitled *A Pluralistic Universe* "The Present Situation in Philosophy," and in the initial chapters he sketches three different religious choices. Theism offers a God "out there" and a basically dualistic account of the universe. Divine human activity is not an illusion; but theism, advocating as it does a God complete from all eternity, "makes us outsiders and keeps us foreigners in relation to God."[28] Since God and truth exist from all time, God does not come to know himself through us; we are merely passive observers. In short, theism does not allow for *possibility*. James explains this by saying that there is no intimacy between creature and creator. The formal structure of theism is such that the possibility of responding to divine invitation does not even logically exist. In theism, "God is not heart of our heart and reason of our reason, but our magistrate, rather; and mechanically to obey his commands, however strange they may be, remains our only moral duty." [29] Theism allows diversity but at – too high a price: loss of any intimacy, loss of interaction, loss of actual possibility.

Pantheism, by contrast, offers us a more intimate relationship with God. The question is, at what price? James distinguishes a more intimate and a less intimate form of pantheism.[30] The monistic form of pantheism, which James calls the "philosophy of the absolute," ultimately advocates a doctrine of internal relations. These relations between creature and creator are so intimate as to abolish all diversity whatsoever as an illusion. In contrast to this "all-form," James delineates an "each-form," that is, a pluralistic pantheism, which "is willing to believe that there may ultimately never be an all-form at all, that the substance of reality may never get totally collected, that some of it may remain outside of the largest combination of it ever made." [31] Most important, James specifically identifies pluralistic pantheism and radical empiricism. "If we give to the monistic subspecies the name of philosophy of the absolute, we may give that of radical empiricism to its pluralistic rival." [32] This identification is of no small importance, for it shows that radical empiricism is *not* neutral on the religious question. This is so because it is through religion as a "faith state" that James preserves actual possibility, though as we shall later see, he sometimes overstates the case for religion.

Logic and Reality

Reflecting on his earlier philosophic position, James recalls that in *The Principles* he could not accept a reductionistic point of view of reality. For example, H_2-plus-0 together produce a new entity, because they *"affect surrounding bodies differently."*[33] Note the use of the pragmatic criterion here: ideas are different if they have different effects. Similarly, James argued that consciousness of the alphabet was *not* reducible to twenty-six separate awarenesses of its specific parts, but that "consciousness of the alphabet . . . [was] a twenty-seventh fact."[34] Analogously, in the religious field, James rejected the idealistic thesis that each of us is a part of a wider consciousness, and that the whole is reducible to the sum of its parts. "If the absolute makes us by knowing us, how can we exist otherwise than *as* it knows us?"[35] This was James's strongest argument against absolute idealism, namely, that it was contrary to our own experience of ourselves as diverse. That is, even if we are only the ideas of the absolute, nonetheless we *appear* to ourselves differently, and this apparent diversity, even illusion, nonetheless exists. This illusion is not explained simply by ignoring it. Alternatively, admitting that there is diversity but stating that the absolute exists in two respects or under two aspects is also not a sufficient explanation. "What boots it to call the parts and the whole the same body of experience, when in the same breath you have to say that the all 'as such' means one sort of experience and each part 'as such' means another?"[36] James then sharpens the focus of his attack: it is not so much the *multum-in-parvo* aspect of the absolute that he denies; it is the relegation of this feature of reality to one *part* of it, *together* with the claim that this outlook is completely rational, that is, that there is nothing "preferred" or "empirically appealing." In actuality, he accuses the idealists of being "masked irrationalists"—at least in part—and suggests that candor is better.

Throughout *A Pluralistic Universe*, one finds indications on James's part that he thought reality more subtle than any formal system. At the very beginning he writes: "No philosophy can ever be anything but a summary sketch, a picture of the world in abridgment, a foreshortened bird's-eye view of the perspective of events."[37] And again, "A philosophy . . . must indeed be true, but that is the least of its requirements."[38] Such a metatheoretical outlook has an essential vagueness or open texture to it. The match-up between formal outlook and reality is not a completely neat one. There is room for possibility, for action. "If we take the whole history of philosophy, the systems reduce themselves to a few main types which, under all the technical verbiage in which the ingenious intellect of man envelops them, are just so many visions, modes of feeling the whole push, and seeing the whole drift of life, forced on one by one's total character and experience, and on the whole *preferred*—there is no other truthful word—as one's best working attitude." [39]

In statements such as these, James has given advance notice of his metaphysical position. That position maintains that reality is not only broader than the known; it is broader than the knowable. Logic, while necessary, is not a sufficient description of reality. His rejection of the sufficiency of logic is strong and clear:

> For my own part, I have finally found myself compelled to *give up the logic,* fairly, squarely, and irrevocably. It has an imperishable use in human life, but that use is not to make us theoretically acquainted with the essential nature of reality. . . . Reality, life, experience, concreteness, immediacy, use what word you will, exceeds our logic, overflows and surrounds it. If you like to employ words eulogistically, as most men do, and so encourage confusion, you may say that reality obeys a higher logic, or enjoys a higher rationality. But I think that even eulogistic words should be used rather to distinguish than to commingle meanings, so I prefer bluntly to call reality if not irrational, then at least non-rational in its constitution. [40]

In a more general fashion, James rejected an overly intellectual approach and, as we shall see in Chapter Four, held that language and concepts per se can give us only aspects of reality. [41] They conceal in the very act of disclosing. James suggests that this overemphasis on intellectualism began as far back as Plato and Socrates, when concepts began to be used "privatively as well as positively,"[42] that is, not only to define reality, but to exclude the undefinable.

In opposition to all this, he espouses a relational metaphysics. Each moment of experience is related positively and negatively, conjunctively and disjunctively, with a series of others, and indirectly with everything else. Important for our purposes here is James's clear delineation of a metaphysic wherein reality is broader than the known, and this is not simply a temporary problematic. "Thought deals . . . solely with surfaces. It can name the thickness of reality, but it cannot fathom it, and its insufficiency here is essential and permanent, not temporary."[43] And again, "The whole process of life is due to life's violation of our logical axioms."[44] What really exists for James "is not things made but things in the making."[45] And this process cannot be completely grasped by language, concepts, or thought itself. Each passing moment is more complex than we have realized, more vague and multidimensional than our concepts can pick up. Not only the absolute but every pulse of experience possesses this common complexity, this vagueness.

The Metatheoretical Level, the Faith Ladder, and Actual Possibility

So far, James has identified radical empiricism as pluralistic pantheism and asserted that reality is broader than the know*able*. What happens at this metatheoretical level when one analyzes James's own philosophic position on its own terms? Here the importance of actual possibility clearly emerges. James realized that his own presentation, while it discloses reality, *at the same time* conceals, that is, is only itself a retrospective presentation, through conceptual symbols. "As long as one continues *talking*, intellectualism remains in undisturbed possession of the field. The return to life can't come about by talking. It is an *act:* to make you return to life, I must . . . deafen you to talk. . . . Or I must *point,* point to the mere *that* of life." [46]

James's most detailed analysis of his own position occurs at the end of *A Pluralistic Universe.* In his concluding remarks, he first of all defines God as in some sense finite; the superhuman consciousness, "however vast it may be, has itself an external environment." [47] This, of course, would be demanded by a metaphysic in which reality is broader than the know*able.* Once this is acknowledged, James argues that the supposed division between a religious rationalism and irreligious empiricism collapses. One can see the divine through the empirical, since each moment of experience is a *"multum in parvo"* [48] relationally constituted in a pluralistic fashion. God is then in time, in history, and so forth, [49] not above them; *"nothing* real escapes from having an environment." [50]

But having added these final touches, James turns to the issue of possibility as being of great concern. First, he shows that, again, his outlook is *not* one merely of atomism. Possibility, in terms of a space of operations, does exist. "Our 'multiverse' still makes a 'universe'; for every part, tho it may not be in actual or immediate connection, is nevertheless in some possible or mediated connection, with every other part however remote, through the fact that each part hangs together with its very next neighbors in inextricable interfusion." [51] And again, "A thing may be connected by intermediary things, with a thing with which it has no immediate or essential connection. It is thus at all times in many possible connections which are not necessarily actualized at the moment." [52] Clearly here, again, James is concerned to preserve possibility. That is, the logical possibility of his viewpoint is necessary, even though not sufficient. James says that the "only thing I emphatically insist upon is that it [pluralistic pantheism] is a fully co-ordinate hypothesis with monism. This world *may,* in the last resort, be a block-universe; but on the other hand, it *may* be a universe only strung-along, not rounded in and closed. Reality *may* exist distributively just as it sensibly seems to, after all. On that possibility I do insist."[53]

Here James is asserting that his position makes logical sense, that it is not meaningless. When compared to monistic idealism, it is a logically possible alternative. But James has also told the reader that the "pragmatic difference between the two systems is . . . a definite one." For an idea to be true pragmatically is for it to be a leading that is worthwhile, to make a difference in our return to the flux of experience, and so on. If one asks the question, What difference does it make pragmatically, if one accepts James's outlook as opposed to monistic idealism? such a question cannot be answered in terms of logical possibility. The alternative to monistic idealism must be meaningful, that is, logically possible, but that is *not* sufficient.

James shows this by referring to the "faith ladder," that is, the way in which we select one conceptual theory over another:

> A conception of the world arises in you somehow, no matter how.
> Is it true or not? you ask.
> It *might* be true somewhere, you say, for it is not self-contradictory.
> It *may* be true, you continue, even here and now.
> It is *fit* to be true, it would be *well if it were true*, it *ought* to be true, you presently feel.
> It *must* be true, something persuasive in you whispers next; and then—as a final result—
> It shall be *held for true*, you decide; it *shall be* as if true, for *you*.
> And your acting thus may in certain special cases be a means of making it securely true in the end.
> Not one step in this process is logical, yet it is the way in which monists and pluralists alike espouse and hold fast to their visions. It is life exceeding logic, it is the

practical reason for which the theoretic reason finds arguments after the conclusion is once there.[54]

Here James overstates his case, but only slightly. In analyzing a philosophical conceptualization, he (or the reader) first realizes that it is logically possible. It is not inherently self-contradictory. Such a move is necessary, but by no means sufficient. Analogously, in *Pragmatism*, an idea must have "meaning" in the linguistic sense of "formal significance," but this is not what James was interested in when he asked, "What does it *mean* pragmatically, to say that an idea is true?" Here the putative philosophical system must have formal logical significance, but reality is such that *many* conceptualizations satisfy this demand. As a result, we still have an indeterminacy and a demand for more radical possibility. This is verbalized strongly by James in the language of the contrary-to-fact conditional: "it would be *well if it were true*." This is clearly actual possibility. In other words, the universe is now so structured that one can say, "Although X (e.g., salvation) is not the case now, it would be the case if each person did his/her level best." Such actualization is clearly more than an empirical statement, in the ordinary sense of empiricism. It describes what is the case in a situation that by definition does not exist. What is important to note is the fact that the faith ladder, used by James as a final description of his position, demands actual possibility. It clearly points out the insufficiency of logic, and it shows that participation, response to a situation, can take place only if actual possibility is affirmed.

The second important thing that James does in this concluding chapter of *A Pluralistic Universe* is to assert that the philosopher's own outlook *itself* becomes part of reality. The situation is reflexive, in the sense of continually growing, changing. "Our philosophies swell the current of being, add their character to it. . . . Our thoughts determine our acts, and our acts redetermine the previous nature of the world."[55] This situation reaffirms the structure of the universe as described in the presentation of the faith ladder. Reality is so constituted that its very ambiguity compels us to respond by formulating philosophical outlooks that will, in the future, alter this now-existing reality. We now know that, in at least some situations, it is possible to "swell the current of being" in a positive humane manner. At this metatheoretic or second-order level, James realizes that his own "preferred" theory is not true but would come about if one acted accordingly. Again, actual possibility is demanded.

Conclusion

This chapter has focused on three themes: first, radical empiricism is specifically identified with pluralistic pantheism, that is, it is not neutral on the question of religion. Second, in James's metaphysics, reality is not only larger than the known, but larger than the know*able*. Reality transcends logic, though the latter is necessary. Third, James offers that reality is such that it compels commitment even in terms of philosophic formulations of it. Several of these are meaningful, that is, logically possible, and James offers that we are forced to select one over another for reasons not completely logical, that is, in terms of the faith ladder.

As in the pragmatism section, this position demands the existence of actual possibility. James did describe himself as an empiricist, but of a radical kind. So much is often emphasized. What is often not noted is that James, acting as an empiricist, did not reject the contrary-to-fact conditional, that is, actual possibility, but did reject that interpretation of it which viewed subjunctive conditionals as repetitive. In other words, he gave up logic as incapable of dealing with possibility.

While James sees the importance of faith here concerning the issue of religion and religious experience, however, this same vision also creates a certain blindness. That is, if the presentation argued for in *A Pluralistic Universe* is correct, *any* metaphysical outlook will involve an element of choice. James presents the debate between pluralistic pantheism and monistic pantheism as one between two equally powerful hypotheses, and therefore as one where the faith ladder comes into play. But his statements concerning the inadequacy of logic, or about philosophical systems being "on the whole preferred," or the assertion that philosophic systems must be true, but that this is the least of their requirements—these statements begin to disclose a more radical dimension to his thought. They do so because these statements are not relegated to the religious domain. Nor are they necessarily relegated to similar "soft" domains such as aesthetics and morals. Differently stated, objectivity or neutrality may not only not be locatable in areas like religion, but may also not be available in such seemingly untouchable areas as science, percepts/concepts and their interrelationship, and language. Here too the vague will predominate, and so, consequently, will the need to choose between options—sometimes for "passionate" or "sentimental" reasons. In the next chapter these three areas are taken up in more detail.

It has also been pointed out in this chapter that James recognized that his own presentation points beyond itself, that it too, as a text, both reveals and conceals. As such the text has to be discussed on two levels. On one level, the text is an invitation to the reader, a suggestion that this is a better way to look at things than alternative ways. As such it is directive, even though it contains some descriptive aspects. But equally important, the text as the expression of its author constitutes part of his continued effort to sustain the will to believe. The "text," in short, is itself an activity. I return to this theme in the Conclusion.

Chapter Three

Vagueness in Science, Percepts, and Language

Science

James is often seen as a somewhat antiscientific philosopher in the American tradition—or at least as scornful of scientific theories. Furthermore, his views on pragmatism are sometimes seen as a form of positivism. This chapter argues against these views. While James himself wrote no complete philosophy of science, he did write an enormous text on psychology. This in itself should lead one to expect that he had some view(s) on scientific procedure. And indeed, this is the case. There exist, scattered throughout James's writing, several references to scientific procedure. When assembled, they offer the beginning of a philosophy of science. Furthermore, his overall outlook is quite antipositivistic in tone.[1]

To begin with, James clearly rejected the old Baconian model of science. While admitting that the compilation of tables of information might be useful at times, he thought it totally unrealistic "to hope that the mere fact of mental confrontation with a certain series of facts" would be "sufficient to make *any* brain conceive their law."[2] The scientific observer was considered by James to be an active transformer of experience, and the "conceiving of a law is a spontaneous variation in the strictest sense of the term."

Scientific laws, then, are more than merely copies; it is therefore quite conceivable that more than one law might account for the same phenomena. Indeed, James points out that it was over this precise issue of multiple conceptual theories that the Baconian model came into times of difficulty. Before 1850 the common belief was that "sciences expressed truths that were exact copies of a definite code of non-human realities."[3] From then on, however, there developed an enormous multiplication of conceptual frameworks. This cast doubt on the opinion that any one of them was a "more literally objective" kind of theory than another. The rising number of geometries, logics, physical and chemical explanations, each in its own way "good for so much and yet not good for everything," militated toward the opinion that "even the truest — formula may be a human device and not a literal transcript." In *The Principles of Psychology*, James sometimes argues in a like vein, speaking out forcefully against the absurdity of the "popular notion that 'Science' is forced on the mind *ab extra,* and that our interests have nothing to do with its constructions."[4] Although these texts are only a beginning, they show that James's view of science allowed for laws to add "something" not given in empirical experience, and for the active participation of the scientist. At the very least, these texts militate against an overly reductionist view of scientific procedure. And indeed, other considerations bear out this opinion.

If James did reject the Baconian model of scientific procedure, what model did he in fact espouse? Speaking in more general epistemological terms in "The Sentiment of Rationality," he offers his own version of the "black box" theory. "The world may in fact be likened unto a lock, whose inward nature, moral or unmoral, will never reveal itself to our simply expectant gaze. The positivists, forbidding us to make any assumptions regarding it, condemn us to eternal ignorance, for the 'evidence' which they wait for can never come so long as we are passive."[5]

Starting with the view that the world is opaque, then, James specifically criticized the passivity of positivism and affirmed the active role of the person in formulating hypotheses. Indeed, in *The Varieties*, James notes that a "good hypothesis in science must have other properties than those of the phenomenon it is immediately invoked to explain, otherwise it is not prolific enough." [6] He believed that the order that could be found in scientific theories was not congruent with the actual state of reality or with the manner in which reality appeared to the viewer.[7] Scientific thought, then, was selective, and essentially so. In scientific theories the plurality of data was broken into "separate essences"; scientific theory is a general conception of existing particulars. Through his or her classifications the scientist leaves "nothing in its natural neighborhood," but rather separates "the contiguous" and joins "what the poles divorce." Going further, James clearly realized the foremost difficulty in upholding the "transforming nature" of scientific laws, and he verbalizes his discomfort in a form of what is now called the "theoretician's dilemma" in the philosophy of science: "Hence the unsatisfactoriness of all our speculations. On the one hand, so far as they retain any multiplicity in their terms, they fail to get us out of the empirical sand-heap world; on the other, so far as they eliminate multiplicity the practical man despises their empty barrenness." [8] In trying to answer this self-imposed dilemma, James develops the view that laws are "approximations." Given that many competing conceptual frameworks may explain empirical phenomena, he seems to view laws as heuristic devices, any one of which might be useful at a given time.[9] He seems quite reluctant, however, completely to reduce conceptual laws to sensory experience. Let us look at his texts in some detail.

Pragmatism is one work where James considers scientific laws to be "approximations." There he tells us that the tremendous rise in the number of scientific laws and formulations has resulted in the opinion that no single theory gives the viewer an absolute transcript of reality, "but that any one of them may from some point of view be useful." Here he considers scientific laws as "only a man-made language, a conceptual shorthand." [10] Precisely be- ～

cause theories are heuristic devices they are susceptible to much choice of expression. Again, in "The Sentiment of Rationality," James reminds us of the incompleteness of all our explanations: "They subsume things under heads wider or more familiar; but the last heads, whether of things or of their connections, are mere abstract genera." [11]

Here James clearly refuses to set up any one conceptual framework as possessing ontological status independent of empirical experience. This indeed is what we might expect, given his pragmatic outlook.

Nevertheless, while it is true that James used the term "approximations" to characterize scientific laws, it would be a mistake to say that he viewed laws as simply reducible to sensory experience. Remember that James himself upheld the thesis that an investigation of the physical universe might well yield a number of formulae, all consistent with the facts.[12] He gives as one example the one-fluid vis-à-vis the two-fluid theory of electricity. How, then, does one select one theory over another if a simple reductionism cannot be performed? In *Pragmatism*, James's answer is in terms of a theory's simplicity or "elegance." [13] He agrees with James Clerk-Maxwell's opinion that it would be in poor scientific taste "to choose the more complicated of two equally well evidenced conceptions." Furthermore, a theory's comportment with both past experience and present novelty must be taken into account. "Truth in science is what gives us the maximum possible sum of satisfactions, taste included, but consistency both with previous truth and with novel fact is always the most imperious claimant." Again, in *The Meaning of Truth*, James tells us that "the suspicion is in the air nowadays that the superiority of one of our formulas to another may not consist so much in its literal 'objectivity,' as in subjective qualities like its usefulness, its 'elegance,' or its congruity with our residual beliefs." [14]

Although James uses the misleading language of subjectivity and objectivity here, it is important to remember that *both* these aspects of experience would be considered real for him. Indeed, he is often accused of giving too much weight to subjective preferences. In the present situation, then, James would seem to be groping toward a position that would see conceptual frameworks as dependent on, yet not reducible to, sensory experience.

One other way in which this comes out is in James's opinion on the ontological status of theoretical entities. Here too he offers a view that scientific concepts are mental instruments.

In *Some Problems of Philosophy*, James points out that the current use of several mutually exclusive concepts in physical sciences is militating toward the opinion that no one of these concepts yields objectivity. This has resulted in the opinion by many physicists that the notions of "matter," "mass," "atom," "ether," "inertia," "force," and so forth are not so much duplicates of hidden realities in nature as mental instruments to handle nature by after-substitution of their scheme. They are, in short, to be considered " 'artifacts,' not revelations." [15]

Again, in *Pragmatism*, James warns the reader against an overly literal interpretation of the universe as constituted by atoms. Scientists may look at the universe "*as if* reality were made of ether, atoms, or electrons," [16] but they should not allow this interpretation to be viewed as literal. Indeed, an entity like "energy" does not refer to anything that is objective. Rather should it be seen as a method of "measuring the surface so as to string their changes on a simple formula."

In the more specific case of theoretical entities, then, James argued as he did concerning scientific laws. No one law or entity was to be given completely independent ontological status. But some caution is needed here regarding theoretical entities, just as caution was required in the case of scientific laws. For here also James refuses completely to reduce the theoretical entities to sensory experience.

In *Essays in Radical Empiricism*, he declares that by far the majority of our knowledge is never completely "nailed down." Furthermore, he gives as a specific example of his meaning ether waves and ions. "Ether-waves . . . are things in which my thoughts will never *perceptually* terminate, but my concepts of them lead me to their very brink, to the chromatic fringes . . . which are their really next effects."[17]

The scientific procedure, then, is more complicated than is usually thought for James. Far from being merely a positivist, he saw that neither scientific laws nor theoretical entities could be simply reduced to sensory reality. As Graham Bird has noted:

> James held . . . that many of the terms in our beliefs, which we might call "theoretical" terms and which he called "ejects," were simply not susceptible of direct face to face confrontation with the facts. The more complex and theoretical our beliefs the less plausible it is to imagine them corresponding to some discoverable fact. . . . To cling to the idea of a correspondence in these cases is simply to distort the procedures by which we verify or falsify, accept or reject, the beliefs in which such terms figure.[18]

Nevertheless, as his version of the theoretician's dilemma statement indicates, James was painfully aware of the inadequacy of setting up a theory as a transcendental spectator, impervious to the flux of experience. He developed a view of science that saw the human being (scientist) playing an active role in conceiving alternative frameworks to account for various phenomena. The "parts" of sensory experience were then replaced by the theoretical entities in a scientific theory.

In short, for James, a collection of sensory data is "rationalized";[19] this process consists in the specific concrete items of the perceptual world's being "assimilated," one by one, to corresponding terms existing in the conceptual series. The scientist then assumes "that the relations intuitively found among the latter are what connect the former too." It was in this way, according to James, that gas pressure was rationalized by being identified with the blows of "hypothetic molecules." The scientist then noticed that the closer the molecules were crowded together, the more frequently the blows on the enclosing walls became. This was followed by the discovery of the precise proportionality of the "crowding with the number of blows," and ultimately in the rationalization of Edme Mariotte's empirical law. Finally, each of the scientist's "transformations of the sense order" is similar to this example—interpretants replace sensations, and in this way sensations "get rationally conceived. To 'explain' means to coordinate, one to one, the *thises* of the perceptual flow with the *whats* of the ideal manifold, whichever it be." While scientific theories must be "capable" of terminating in experience, James is careful to point out the importance of elegance, of agreement with past assumptions—as being partially responsible for the acceptance of any theory.

Perhaps the most detailed and sophisticated model of the scientific procedure James gives us is in the last chapter of *The Principles of Psychology*. There he speaks as follows:

> The most persistent outer relations which science believes in are never matters of experience at all, but have to be disengaged from under experience by a process of elimination, that is, by ignoring conditions which are always present. The *elementary* laws of mechanics, physics, and chemistry are all of this sort. The principle of uniformity in nature is of this sort; it has to be *sought* under and in spite of the most rebellious appearances; and our conviction of its truth is far more like a religious faith than like assent to a demonstration. The only cohesions which experience in the literal sense of the word produces in our mind are . . . the proximate laws of nature, and habitudes of concrete things, that heat melts ice, that salt preserves meat, that fish die out of water, and the like. Such "empirical truths" as these we admitted to form an enormous part of human wisdom. The "scientific" truths have to harmonize with these truths, or be given up as useless; but they

arise in the mind in no such passive associative way as that in which the simpler truths arise. Even those experiences which are used to prove a scientific truth are for the most part artificial experiences of the laboratory gained after the truth itself has been conjectured. Instead of experiences engendering the "inner relations," the inner relations are what engender the experiences here.[20]

Here James comes closest to distinguishing not only facts and theories, but facts, laws (empirical generalizations), and theories. He realizes again that the scientific procedure is not passive, but more important, he sees theories as having to harmonize with empirical generalizations but not as being reducible to them.

To be sure, James developed no complete philosophy of science. Nonetheless, there exist several texts where he refers to science. These texts, when taken together, suggest the following tentative conclusions:

1. His constant espousal of the active role of the scientist precludes appeal to any "neutral court of factual data." (In connection with this, it is well to recall that in *Pragmatism* James refused to set up any single discipline—scholasticism, common sense, or science—as the final judge of "making a difference.")[21]

2. He realized that physical data could be dealt with scientifically only via the use of laws or theories not derivable from experience. He nonetheless apparently considered theories to be a necessary precondition of science.

3. He clearly realized that different conceptual formulations could explain the same empirical phenomena; yet he refused to reduce several theories to a single one or completely to reduce the conceptual formulations to empirical data. Indeed, he maintained that all these differ-

ent formulations were real in terms of their effects—their use. Though James is not clear enough here, nonetheless his position seems to militate against the positivist absolute bifurcation of propositions into either tautologies or empirically verifiable statements, vis-à-vis "emotive utterances."

In short, James saw scientific theories as dependent on, yet not reducible to, sensory experience. This position on science parallels his view of the relations of concepts and percepts. An analysis of the Jamesian texts indicates that (1) James refuses to distinguish clearly sensation, percept, and concept; (2) he recognizes the ontological status of concepts (i.e., he was not simply a positivist); and (3) he uses the word "perceptual" in two different ways. This twofold use of the word has been the source of much difficulty; also, it forces us to deal with the issue of James's opinion of language. Here he is often thought of as a romanticist, as someone who believed that life was beyond all language. I shall try to show that this view is at least partly wrong and that there exist two different views of language in the James texts—though James himself sometimes underestimates the tenacity of language.

The Ontological Status of Percepts and Concepts

To begin with, James, in *The Principles*, distinguishes between knowledge-by-acquaintance and knowledge-about, giving as examples the difference in French between *connaître* and *savoir*, in Latin between *noscere* and *scire*, and so forth.[22] Knowledge-by-acquaintance is immediate; knowledge-about, mediate. Knowledge-about is the result of analyzing an object known by direct acquaintance, the classification of an object under a general category. Knowledge-by-acquaintance is more simple than knowledge-about. But since simple is a relative term, it follows that "the same thought of a thing may be called knowledge-about it in comparison with a simpler thought, or acquaintance with it in comparison with a thought of it that is more articulate and explicit still."[23] Apparently, then, knowledge-by-acquaintance is direct, immediate, unanalyzed; knowledge-about, indirect, mediate, and the result of classification; and this distinction varies from context to context. As Seigfried has noted, "even in bare acquaintance, there is still a vague awareness of a fringe of unarticulated affinities."[24] In volume 2 of *The Principles*, James uses this distinction to differentiate between sensation and perception. The closer an object cognized comes to being a simple quality, like hot or cold or red, the closer the state of mind comes to being a pure sensation.[25] Perception, in contrast, includes sensation: "*Sensation . . . differs from Perception only in the extreme simplicity of its object or content. Its function is that of mere acquaintance with a fact. Perception's function, on the other hand, is knowledge about a fact; and this knowledge admits of numberless degrees of complication.*"[26]

Sensations are, then, more simple and more vivid; perceptions, less vivid, more mediate. In *Some Problems of Philosophy*, however, James confuses the issue by using this same yardstick to distinguish percepts from concepts. Percepts are immediate, concepts are mediate.[27] Furthermore, James here gives sensation as a synonym for perception.[28] It would seem, then, that he sometimes made a twofold distinction, sometimes a threefold distinction, all the while using the criteria of knowledge-by-acquaintance as opposed to knowledge-about. The fact that he did not clearly distinguish among sensation, perception, and conception would seem to indicate that the distinction could be made only in a relative manner. Indeed, he has told us above that the distinction between knowledge-by-acquaintance and knowledge-about was only a relative one. If his yardstick itself was not clear, it would follow that his distinctions among sensation, perception, and conception were also relative. In a footnote in *The Principles*, he clearly recognizes the relativity of his distinction between sensations and perceptions: "Some persons will say that we never have a really simple object or content. My definition of sensation does not require the simplicity to be absolutely, but only relatively, extreme."[29] Strictly speaking, then, a pure sensation is an abstraction.[30] All sensations are preperceived, the only persons possibly capable of pure sensations being infants. Since "it is impossible to draw any sharp line of distinction between the barer and the richer consciousness,"[31] a pure perception is also an abstraction. So too are pure concepts abstract: "To understand life by concepts is to arrest its movement, cutting it up into bits . . . and immobilizing these in our logical herbarium where, comparing them as dried specimens, we can ascertain which of them statically includes or excludes which other."[32]

Apparently, then, while James made *theoretical* distinctions among sensations, perceptions, and conceptions, he did not believe that these distinctions were absolute. Reality could not be neatly divided into three (or two) parts. Each of these—sensations, perceptions, or conceptions—when taken by itself, was a vicious abstraction. In the real world no clear distinction can be made among these three. This is so because the criteria being used are relative. What is knowledge-about in one instance may be knowledge-by-acquaintance in another, and this in respect to all three entities. If no clear distinction can be made, and no reduction is possible, we have no choice but to view all of these as interpenetrating "aspects" of reality. James explicitly tells us that a reduction is impossible. Percepts and concepts must be seen as melting into one another; neither of these, taken alone, gives us a complete picture of reality. In *Some Problems of Philosophy*, he says: "No careful reader of my text will accuse me of identifying 'knowledge' with either perception or conception absolutely or exclusively. Perception gives 'intention,' conception gives 'extention' to our knowledge."[33] Far from being mere abstractions, concepts play a vital role. They enable us to steer through experience by providing us with a map of relations.[34] In addition, they cause us to revalue life by making our action turn on new points of emphasis. "With concepts we go in quest of the absent, meet the remote, actively turn this way or that, . . . change its [experience's] order, run it backwards, bring far bits together and separate near bits, . . . string its items on as many ideal diagrams as our mind can frame. . . . We *harness* perceptual reality in concepts in order to drive it better to our ends." [35] In short, the conceptual maps framed by the mind would seem to possess some independent existence, since they can be neither ignored nor reduced. Nevertheless, concepts cannot be taken as exclusively "real." There are several "maps" or several opinions as to the essence of any given object. All classification is teleological. We determine the essence of an object as "that one of its properties which is so *important for my interests* that in comparison with it I may neglect the rest." [36] The conceptual realm contains an infinite number of frameworks, but these exist as possibilities, to be selected by us in terms of our needs and interests. The real world for James is a processive one, in which both concepts and percepts (or concepts, percepts, and sensations) have ontological status. We preperceive the present moment through the concepts of the past; the latter cannot be "reduced" to the present or wished away as mere rational abstractions.

If the analysis above is correct, we might well ask the question, Why does James himself call the real world the *perceptual world*? Indeed, he has told us time and again that sensation and apperceptive ideas fuse, with the result that "you can no more tell where one begins and the other ends, than you can tell, in those cunning circular panoramas, . . . where the real foreground and the painted canvas join together." [37] Why, then, the insistence on labeling his metaphysical outlook as perceptual? One explanation might be the following: Concepts are defined by their exclusivity. It is only as something is recognized as a that-and-no-other that it is termed a "concept." As James says, "The great difference between percepts and concepts is that percepts are continuous and concepts are discrete." [38] Concepts are "cuts" made into the ongoing experience, for the purpose of running ahead and predicting possible outcomes. As such, they must return to, must terminate in, the world of sensible experience. The latter is termed more real by James because it is more vivid and because it is not exclusive. In *The Principles*, he says: "As a whole, sensations are more lively and are judged more real than conceptions." [39] This text, however, should be taken in conjunction with one in *Some Problems of Philosophy*: "The manyness-in-oneness which perception offers is impossible to construe intellectually." [40] Taking the two statements together, we see that the perceptual world is richer and more intense than the conceptual one, and *therefore* it is termed more real. Again, no sheer reductionism can be performed. Reality consists of interpenetrating sensations, perceptions, and conceptions. To say this linguistically is already to make an unwarranted division. I shall take up the problem of language forthwith. For the present, let us note that James is dissatisfied with the linguistic exclusivity of concepts. Yet James is forced to use concepts to articulate a view of experience wherein certain aspects must be taken as interpenetrant—but this cannot be clearly said linguistically: "Whatever we distinguish and isolate conceptually is found perceptually to telescope and compenetrate and diffuse into its neighbors." [41] The perceptual world is the "real" one because it is defined as nonexclusive, thereby allowing for more richness, and because it is concerned with one's feelings, thereby allowing for intensity. Most important, it is capable of allowing these two to exist together. In this way we might say that "perceptual" is used in two different senses in James's works. In the narrower sense it is the conceptual alternative to conceptions. In the wider sense the "perceptual" realm includes the conceptual. In conclusion, both percepts and concepts are real for James. No clear distinction and no reduction is admissible. But the real world that contains percepts and concepts is better termed "perceptual" because the latter term is inclusive of conceptual, while "conceptual" stands for exclusivity. But even this way of posing the problematic "masks" an important issue: namely, how the two uses of "perceptual" are related, or in other terms, to what extent language points beyond itself toward reality, rather than just describing the latter. In addition, there remains the issue of to what degree language can, or cannot, be done away with.

The fact that James used images such as the "landscape panorama" indicates that he was aware of the linguistic difficulty here. Indeed, Seigfried has argued that for James, "analogical thinking is actually an indispensable constituent of all thinking and not a disposable relic of a more primitive era." [42] James, then, is incorrectly viewed as a romantic who thought that language was at best unimportant and at worst downright encumbersome to his philosophical views, though he is at times frustrated with language. There actually exist two different views on language in the Jamesian texts. One of these is disparaging toward language, but the second is surprisingly contemporary.

Language

The First Position

The first position on language is the one most readily identified with James, and it is found scattered throughout his works. In *The Principles*, for example, he states that "language works against our perception of the truth. We name our thoughts simply, each after its thing, as if each knew its own thing and nothing else. What each really knows is clearly the thing it is named for, with dimly perhaps a thousand other things." [43] Here James argues that we all take language too much for granted. We all assume that each word has one meaning and that when the word is used in n number of sentences, the meaning is the same. Language so taken, he asserts, is inadequate to the substantive and transitive parts of the stream of consciousness. The sheer inadequacy of language to describe the nuances of the stream is brought out by James in *The Principles*. Having asserted that relations between things are real, both in the real order of events and in the stream of consciousness, he continues:

There is not a conjunction or a preposition, and hardly
an adverbial phrase, syntactic form, or inflection of voice,
in human speech, that does not express some shading
or other of relation which we at some moment actually
feel to exist between the larger objects of our thought. If
we speak objectively, it is the real relations that appear
revealed; if we speak subjectively, it is the stream of consciousness that matches each of them by an inward color-
ing of its own. In either case the relations are numberless,
and no existing language is capable of doing justice to all
their shades.[44]

Language simply cannot grasp the transitive parts—it either
overlooks them or substantializes them; in either case they are not
recognized as such. This realization leads James at times to reject
language. "Language is the most imperfect and expensive means
yet discovered for communicating thought."[45] And again, "What
an awful trade that of professor is—paid to talk, talk, talk! I have
seen artists growing pale and sick whilst I talked to them without
being able to stop. . . . It would be an awful universe if *everything* could be converted into words, words, words."[46] In short,
these texts present language as too sluggish. Words, like abstract
concepts, are too linear; a sentence turns out to be a set of building blocks. Each part can be separated and does not necessarily
affect its neighbor. When James took language "at face value,"
he found it woefully inadequate; a statue, it froze the ongoing
flux of experience. More important, the disjunctions and conjunctions of discourse were considered to be merely neutral logical
connectives. As such, language insulates us from dimensions of
processive experience, rather than serving as a wedge into the
tissue of experience for "pragmatic" purposes. As Graham Bird
has noted:

It was an error due to language which James holds responsible for the faulty atomism of traditional empiri-

cists. There is a natural tendency to cut our stream of consciousness into discrete fragments corresponding to the substantive parts of the stream which we attend to and name. He thinks that such features of language mislead us quite generally, in encouraging us to believe that some thing corresponds to every name and that the absence of a name entails the absence of any discriminable feature. In this general way he echoes Wittgenstein's therapeutic claim that we ascribe to the object what belongs to our method of projection in the language.[47]

Not everything James wrote about language was negative, however. He was quite willing to admit that we need labels to find our way about. If one could successfully label an encountered object, it could be subsumed in the right system, and its properties immediately known. Indeed, this is the way most of us function. *"The only things which we commonly see are those which we preperceive . . .* which have been labeled for us. . . . If we lost our stock of labels we should be intellectually lost in the midst of the world."[48]

Here James clearly realizes that language cannot be merely "thrown overboard." Language is quite important because of its close connection with conceptualization. It was one means of enabling persons to contain vicariously large amounts of their past experience and therefore of enabling them to deal with a novel situation. The only remaining alternative open for James is to construct a different theory of language.

The Second Position

Although no complete theory of language exists in James's work, nonetheless there does exist a host of "positive" statements that would constitute a good beginning for a linguistic framework. Specifically, James recognized that meanings vary from context to context; he was cognizant of the intentional (or "leading") aspect of discourse; he saw some sentences as essentially directional rather than merely descriptive; and he renounced the view of language as substantive words strung together by neutral logical connectives.

To begin with, James was quite opposed at times to the idea of one word having one meaning, irrespective of contextual nuances. He suggests that if "language must . . . influence us, the agglutinative languages, and even Greek and Latin with their declensions, would be the better guides. Names did not appear in them inalterable, but changed their shape to suit the context in which they lay." [49] James presents the reader with several examples of linguistic "contextual importance" in his works. In *The Principles*, he says:

> When I use the word *man* in two different sentences, I may have both times exactly the same sound upon my lips and the same picture in my mental eye, but I may mean, and at the very moment of uttering the word and imagining the picture, know that I mean, two entirely different things. Thus when I say: "What a wonderful man Jones is!" I am perfectly aware that I mean by man to exclude Napoleon Bonaparte or Smith. But when I say: "What a wonderful thing Man is!" I am equally well aware that I mean to *in*clude not only Jones, but Napoleon and Smith as well. [50]

This quotation develops both the intentional and contextual aspects of language. In either case a main point seems to be that language is not an objective copy of reality. It does not exist as an "object" at all—a much more subtle relationship, an overlapping one among subject, language, and reality, would seem more adequate. There is a sense in which a person creates reality by naming it, by molding it linguistically. This may pose new problems, but it renders inadequate the doctrine that the only purpose of language is the impartial description of events.

Another example is the text in *Pragmatism* where James tries to articulate the meaning of a statement such as "The world is One":

> Granting the oneness to exist, what facts will be different in consequence? . . . Many distinct ways in which a oneness predicated of the universe might make a difference, come to view . . . 1. . . . [as] *one subject of discourse* . . . 2. [as] *continuous* . . . 3. . . . Lines of *influence* can be traced by which they hang together . . . 4. [in terms of] *causal unity* . . . 5. [as] *generic unity* . . . 6. [in terms of] *unity of purpose* . . . 7. [as] *Aesthetic union*, 8. [in terms of] *one* Knower. . . . "The world is One," therefore, just so far as we experience it to be concatenated. One by as many definite conjunctions as appear. But then also *not* One by just as many definite *disjunctions* as we find. . . . It is neither a universe pure and simple nor a multiverse pure and simple.[51]

The meaning of "one" is not univocal for James, nor is it simply equivocal; there exists rather concatenated "family resemblances" among all of the above meanings of "one," but a reductionism cannot be performed. The only way to ascertain the meaning of "one" is contextually. The emphasis is on richness as opposed to reductionism. Ellen Suckiel has noted this point also:

> For James, as for Wittgenstein later in the century, the meaning of an idea is not separable from the context of its use. To articulate the meaning of an idea is not to rehearse a list of other logically equivalent ideas; it is to use that idea as a tool in the context of particular concrete problems and concerns. As Wittgenstein was to hold that it is misguided to search for the meaning of a word outside of that word's own language-game, James holds that abstracting concepts out of their particular uses, and

treating those abstractions by themselves as significant, are bound to result in sterility and confusion.[52]

The importance of context is closely aligned with a second aspect of James's positive views on language—the fact that language has a leading function to perform and, more important, that this cannot be divorced from the word, or the sentence, as the case may be. "Names are just as 'true' or 'false' as definite mental pictures are. They set up similar verification-processes, and lead to fully equivalent practical results."[53] James expresses this same view in a slightly different manner in *The Principles*, where he notes the leading or directive function of language. "The feeling of an absence is *toto coelo* other than the absence of a feeling . . . [L]arge tracts of human speech are nothing but *signs of direction* in thought, of which direction we nevertheless have an acutely discriminative sense, though no definite sensorial image plays any part in it whatsoever."[54] Language, then, is directive and it must be so viewed. Each word, each sentence, points beyond itself—it is "leading." James quotes Joubert approvingly on this subject: "We only know just what we meant to say, after we have said it."[55]

There is, in brief, a vagueness about language, vagueness in the sense of our not knowing what we wanted to say until we have said it. Language does not exist impartially or objectively. We find ourselves involved with it, with the immediate result that we choose certain words without knowing for sure what they mean or, in James's words, where they will lead. As I speak, I am conscious of each word running ahead of itself, feeling at home in the context, or not, as the case may be. A word-in-this-context is not the same as a word-in-that-context, but it is not completely different either. There is a richness about words; they can stand for this *or* that *or* the other, and most important, the "or's" are not exclusive. Language is rich because it is intense, and vice versa. Like consciousness, it is a sliding focalization, continuous and selective.

> There is about each word the psychic "overtone" of feeling that it brings us nearer to a forefelt conclusion. . . . Each word, in . . . a sentence, is felt, not only as a word, but as having a *meaning*. The "meaning" of a word taken thus dynamically in a sentence may be quite different from its meaning when taken statically or without context. The dynamic meaning is . . . the bare fringe . . . of felt suitability or unfitness to the context and conclusion. The static meaning, when the word is concrete, as "table," "Boston," consists of sensory images awakened; when it is abstract, as "criminal legislation," "fallacy," the meaning consists of other words aroused, forming the so-called "definition." [56]

Taken statically, then, words have what we might call possible leadings. But the basic way to take words is dynamically, as signs of direction. As such they point beyond the simple definition or conception toward the situation they are used in. This "fringe" is conceptually opaque, so we tend to ignore it and to pay attention only to a word and its meaning; or in other words, we succumb to what James called "vicious intellectualism." [57] To do this is to abstract out of the primary mode of linguistic experience.

From this perspective each word is a focalization surrounded by a fringe. Going further, we see that not only words, but sentences, are focalizations. If language is best articulated as a focus/ fringe directional continuum, then the atomistic view of sentences being built up of pieces, nouns and verbs having a value of "1," and connectives being valued at "0," is wrong. The substantive and the transitive parts have to be taken into account. As James says, "The word 'or' names a genuine reality." [58] Again, this point is brought out in *The Principles of Psychology*: "We ought to say a feeling of *and,* a feeling of *if,* a feeling of *but,* and a feeling of *by,* quite as readily as we say a feeling of *blue* or a feeling of *cold.*" [59] Finally, in *Essays in Radical Empiricism*, James states: "Prepositions, copulas, and conjunctions, 'is,' 'isn't,' 'then,' 'before,' 'in,' 'on,' 'beside,' 'between,' 'next,' 'like,' 'unlike,' 'as,' 'but,' flower out of the stream of pure experience, the stream of concretes or the sensational stream, as naturally as nouns and adjectives do, and they melt into it again as fluidly when we apply them to a new portion of the stream."[60] In brief, for James, all the sections of a sentence are real, as all the sections of consciousness were; furthermore, they are not really separate sections at all. "The *Object* of your thought is really its entire content or deliverance, neither more nor less. It is a vicious use of speech to take out a substantive kernel from its content and call that its object; and it is an equally vicious use of speech to add a substantive kernel not articulately included in its content, and to call that its object."[61] The entire content includes, of course, the intention and the leading or directional aspect of the sentence. It also includes both substantive and transitive parts of discourse.

In sum, language, like life, is ongoing, unfinished; as such it has a "vagueness" about it. James occasionally senses this and at times tries to articulate it. Nevertheless, language is often taken (even by James) as being chopped up, static, and fixed. When James does take language in this second way, he is extremely critical of its inadequacy to do justice to the richness and intensity of experience. But there are times when the positive tone prevails and we receive "sketches" of a much more dynamic view of language. In addition, one must always keep in mind the fact that James himself is using language and for the most part is quite conscious of this. Language is for him a continuation of the battle of life "felt as a real fight"; in addition, the language of James's text exists as a provocation to the reader.[62]

Conclusion

James's position on percepts/concepts parallels his philosophy of science. In both areas conceptual formulations are dependent on, yet not reducible to, sensory experience. James's position on the ontological status of percepts and concepts appears ambiguous at first sight, however. This is so because he uses "perceptual" in two ways, as the theoretical (i.e., exclusive) alternative to "conceptual" and as inclusive of "conceptual." This twofold use of the word "perceptual" prompted an investigation of his views on language. Sometimes, for James, language, where language is taken as static, is deemed inadequate. But at other times a dynamic view of language—not unlike that of later Wittgenstein—can be seen in his works. At any rate, James can be termed neither a positivist pure and simple nor a romantic intuitionist. In the final analysis his thought remains richer than these categories.

The difficulty James had with language and his twofold use of the term "perceptual" are reflected and intensified in his metaphysics of "pure experience," to which we now turn.

Chapter Four

James's Metaphysics: Language as the "House of 'Pure Experience' "

Several times during this century James has been "discovered" by proponents of "European" philosophy. Both the Continental and the Anglo-Saxon traditions have attempted to show affinities between his outlook and theirs. In *The Origins of Pragmatism*, A. J. Ayer views James as a strong phenomenalist, with some strong similarities to his own position.[1] The phenomenological tradition has not lacked authors devoted to the thesis that there exist strong affinities between James's views and their own. Thus James Edie has termed James a "proto-phenomenologist;"[2] Ellen Suckiel has agreed, saying that "the most appropriate designation for his [James's] view as it applies to physical objects is that it is a protophenomenology: common-sense objects as constituted by the subject within lived experience are the ultimately real physical objects of our world."[3] Bruce Wilshire has highlighted the strong phenomenological stance in *The Principles of Psychology*;[4] and Richard Stevens has shown that, given certain conditions, there exist strong similarities between James's outlook and Edmund Husserl's.[5]

In such a situation, the question naturally arises, Whose interpretation is right? And as in most philosophical debates, there probably is no completely satisfactory answer. There are dimensions in James's thought which do not fit neatly into either of the two traditions. A very important case must be made for James as representative of an indigenous "American angle of vision," philosophically speaking.[6]

Here we concentrate primarily on the two "European" interpretations. Rather than adding one more argument to one side or the other, let us attempt to "transcend" the issue by adopting the following stratagem: one item that both traditions have always held in high esteem is language. To be sure, William James had no complete theory of language. Nonetheless, as we have seen, there do exist, scattered throughout the Jamesian corpus, several statements on language. Actually, these statements indicate a two-level position. Sometimes James viewed language negatively, as insulating rather than liberating. But at other times he viewed language more positively, as necessary, albeit inadequate, to deal with reality. In these latter statements he views language as contextual, as unfinished, and as pointing beyond itself.[7]

What are the implications of this view for James's metaphysics and for his supposed affinities with phenomenology or phenomenalism? First, since language, when used positively, is contextual, no apodictic description, no foundation is available. As we shall see later, reality cannot be completely "bracketed." This would seem to rule out at least one form of phenomenology. James's positive view of language, however, presents the latter as pointing beyond itself toward a reality never quite known. Far from reality being a construct out of sensory data as in phenomenalism, just the opposite is the case. James is a "radical realist." Being can be alluded to, pointed toward, but not completely captured in speech.

As is well known, in *The Principles of Psychology*, James adopted a functional dualism, between psychology and philosophy, or thought and reality. His description of consciousness as selective and intentional was a "nascent attack" on the subject/object dichotomy, however. For several years after, James struggled with the issue of how to reject this dualistic division.

His answer, tentative as it is, is contained in *Essays in Radical Empiricism*. For it is here that James introduces the notion of "pure experience."

Let us commence by recalling exactly what "radical empiricism" is, as James himself verbalized it in the preface to *The Meaning of Truth*:

> Radical empiricism consists first of a postulate, next of a statement of fact, and finally of a generalized conclusion.
>
> The postulate is that the only things that shall be debatable among philosophers shall be things definable in terms drawn from experience. . . .
>
> The statement of fact is that the relations between things, conjunctive as well as disjunctive, are just as much matters of direct particular experience, neither more so nor less so, than the things themselves.
>
> The generalized conclusion is that therefore the parts of experience hold together from next to next by relations that are themselves parts of experience. The directly apprehended universe needs, in short, no extraneous trans-empirical connective support, but possesses in its own right a concatenated or continuous structure.[8]

In *Essays in Radical Empiricism*, James asserts that reality is richer than we have realized; it contains not only substantive parts but also transitive ones, and the latter may be of either a disjunctive or a conjunctive nature. In short, at first glance it seems that James extends his analysis of the stream of consciousness (as found in *The Principles of Psychology*) to the stage where it describes reality in general. Indeed, there is much truth in this; a great deal that James has to say about consciousness as a continuously changing stream with all sorts of relational fringes, he also has to say about reality in *Essays in Radical Empiricism*. An overly hasty conclusion might well be that reality *is* consciousness or, less hasty but still wrong, that consciousness is the foundation for this description of reality.

But James, having asserted that for anything to be considered in philosophy it must be capable of being experienced, now asks, How is consciousness experienced? And he gives a pragmatic answer. To the question, What difference does it make if I say "*A* is conscious of *B*" as opposed to "*A* is next to *B*"? James replies: *A* is conscious of *B* if and only if there are a series of intimate, conjunctive transitions between the intermediaries of *A* and *B*, through which *A* goes, saying "ah ha," "yes," "yes," "ah ha," and so on, until he or she reaches the stage of having a vague intention fulfilled, of actually "seeing" that which he or she had in mind.[9] Consciousness, in short, is a function for James; it is not a substance. It is the function of an intimate, agreeable leading. Most important, it is not found as separate at the primary level of experience, but rather arises retrospectively as an addition. The present moment is not simply conscious; it becomes conscious insofar as it is affiliated with other moments in the past.

We must remember that no dualism of being represented and representing resides in the experience *per se*. In its pure state, or when isolated, there is no self-splitting of it into consciousness and what the consciousness is "of." Its subjectivity and objectivity are functional attributes solely, realized only when the experience is "taken" i.e., talked-of, twice, considered along with its two differing contexts respectively, by a new retrospective experience, of which that whole past complication now forms the fresh content.

The instant field of the present is at all times what I call the "pure" experience. It is only virtually or potentially either object or subject as yet.[10]

This text carries several important points. First of all, the subject/object distinction, or the consciousness/content distinction, does not arise at the primordial level of experience, but can be ascertained only by turning from or "bracketing" reality, defined here as the present. When reality is so bracketed, then the relation between consciousness and its object can be described, as has been done above, in terms of intimate conjunctive transitions. Furthermore, there is a "relativism" involved here; what functions as consciousness in one context might well function as the object of consciousness in another context. A given moment of experience can be counted twice over after it drops into the past; it can function both as consciousness and as content of consciousness. It follows from this position that we are never immediately conscious *that* we are conscious, or in other words, that we are never immediately self-conscious. Consciousness of self, like consciousness of any other object-for-consciousness, is only retrospectively available.

So far, the similarities between James and phenomenology seem quite obvious. But the bracketing of reality must be returned to. What of James's own analysis of the situation? What of "radical empiricism" or "pure experience" itself? Has James given the transcendental conditions for consciousness, or is his own outlook *itself* retrospective, even at this level? And if so, what are the implications of this?

The second alternative does indeed appear a more adequate portrayal of the Jamesian outlook; indeed, we have seen him begin to develop such a position in *A Pluralistic Universe* in Chapter Two, above. James was sympathetic with Kierkegaard's statement that "We live forwards . . . but we understand backwards." [11] The situation is no different, and is indeed crucially important, at the metaphysical level. And it is precisely here that James's views on language provide a key insight. As he noted in the quotation above, the subject/object distinction arises only when experience is talked of. Though language is necessary, there is a sense in which language betrays. This is particularly true when one is trying to allude to the question of reality, or in James's terms, to pure experience. With some suspicions of language in mind, then, let us turn to James's portrayals of pure experience. In "Does 'Consciousness' Exist?" James says: "My thesis is that if we start with the supposition that there is only one primal stuff or material in the world, a stuff of which everything is composed, and if we call that stuff 'pure experience,' then knowing can easily be explained as a particular sort of relation towards one another into which portions of pure experience may enter." [12] Elsewhere in *Essays in Radical Empiricism* he tells us that the "principle of pure experience is . . . a methodological postulate." [13]

The statement that there was one "stuff" of experience was to cause James trouble, but even by the end of the article he had anticipated this, telling the reader that he had so spoken only for the sake of fluency and that "there is no *general* stuff of which experience at large is made. There are as many stuffs as there are 'natures' in the things experienced." [14] James's intent seems clear, though his verbalizations of it are causing him difficulty. Pure experience here is neither a "many" nor a "one," but is rather the state of the universe before these two emerge as alternatives. In *Pragmatism*, James has the same problem: he cannot accept monism and so terms his own outlook pluralistic—almost by default. But actually, as he sometimes realized, his own outlook is, again, neither a monism nor a pluralism, but rather a view of reality as "concatenated." [15] Similar difficulties arise with the attempt to verbalize pure experience as beneath the consciousness/content distinction, the percept/concept distinction,[16] and the past/present/future distinction, as we shall see below. In short, James, having asserted the existence of something beneath these various dichotomies, is having great difficulty "catching" it in language. Nevertheless, he must say something; he must be careful not to let pure experience lapse into a supernatural entity or a transcendental category. A strong tenet of radical empiricism is that all things termed "existing" be experienceable. We return to this issue of describing pure experience below.

In the quotations above James views pure experience as a "thesis" and a "methodological postulate." Clearly, then, his metaphysical outlook is not foundationalist in tone and this (nonfoundational) aspect is essential. There is no apodictic ground to the Jamesian outlook. *Even his own position* is to be taken as a hypothesis.

If no foundation can be claimed, should "pure experience"

then be accepted merely as a heuristic device, as an upper case limit, so to speak? This indeed is the approach taken by A. J. Ayer. While admitting that James probably did claim that pure experience is all that there is, Ayer holds that "interpreted in this way, the thesis is very dubious indeed.

To begin with, it is not clear what a claim of this kind amounts to, outside the framework of a given system." [17] With this strong emphasis on meaning, Ayer asserts:

> It may well be that the best course is to take no ontological decisions at all. If we adopt this policy, we shall construe questions about the reality of different sorts of objects only as asking whether the statements which figure in different types of theory are true. . . . [I]f we are able to determine which statements at each of these levels are true and how statements of different kinds are related to each other, there are no matters of truth or falsehood left to be decided. . . . In dissenting from James on this aspect of his thesis that experience is the primal stuff of the world, I have taken a pragmatic view of ontology. [18]

Whatever the merits of this outlook on its own grounds, James would surely have found it unacceptable. First, it implies the traditional positivist clear distinction between the meaningful and the meaningless; and indeed, Ayer in other places divides James's writings into moral/theological on the one hand and epistemological on the other. [19] But in *Pragmatism*, James specifically rejected such a dichotomy; he viewed his new method as a mediator between the tough-minded and the tender-minded. [20] Hence Graham Bird is correct in his assertion that Ayer's "account is misleading in its suggestion that James drew a totally sharp distinction between moral and scientific beliefs. For this overlooks the fact that James regarded emotional satisfaction as important even in the scientific case." [21] Furthermore, James's views on language indicate a contextualist position where the line between meaningful and meaningless cannot be clearly drawn. A second aspect of James's position which would argue strongly against Ayer's interpretation is James's critique of "vicious intellectualism."[22] Here James clearly rejects the reduction or reification of meaning to the stage where the meaning of meaning is constituted by formal semantics. In James's positive linguistic views, meaning included intention (what I want or need) and effect (the practical results of a given idea or statement). Usually, he is criticized for not distinguishing them clearly, but it may well be the case that James believed that no such distinction could be made, at least in any complete sense.

For these reasons, James would not accept the notion that pure experience had meaning only insofar as it was considered true or false within the confines of some specific linguistic system. More and more, James became suspicious of language, especially in its most reified form—logic. So while it is necessary to point out that "pure experience" is not grounded on an apodictic foundation, it is also necessary to reject the interpretation of pure experience as merely a convenient device, necessary to posit but then eminently forgettable.

"Pure experience" is a postulate but it is so in a very *realistic* sense; it points beyond itself. Metaphysically speaking, reality is broader than the known; pure experience represents an attempt by James to get at, or disclose, being. The latter is not an object, since pure experience describes an ontological situation that is prior to the subject/object dichotomy. "Pure experience" is a concept that refers to pure experience in the same way that, for Paul Tillich, "God" is a symbol for God. A symbol, for Tillich, "points beyond itself while participating in that to which it points."[23] Gerald Myers is correct, then, to have "emphasized the pictorial, visionary character of James's concept of pure experience."[24] Actually, the term "pure experience" is used in different, overlapping ways by James. Let us flesh out some of its meanings.

"The instant field of the present is at all times what I call the 'pure experience.'"[25] James often uses this description when he is emphasizing the indeterminate given, existing prior to various dualisms that arise, such as the subject/object and consciousness/content distinctions. Similar statements are: "Experience in its immediacy seems perfectly fluent";[26] and " 'Pure experience' is the name which I gave to the immediate flux of life which furnishes the material to our later reflection with its conceptual categories."[27] Here James tries to portray what is immediately given, but the irony is, what is immediately given is not immediate—it is flux, and qua flux it is the "ground" of all future statements. The present moment is really the passing moment.[28] As Eugene Fontinell has said:

> While everyone might agree that what is immediately experienced is beyond dispute, it is quite evident that just what it is that is immediately experienced is a matter of great dispute. This is made obvious by the variety of competing, inconsistent, and even contradictory claims of immediate experience. James and a host of twentieth-century phenomenologists have significantly deepened our awareness of how difficult it is to describe with complete fidelity the characteristics of experience. There would be no such difficulty if immediate experience were clear, distinct, and unambiguous instead of being characterized by obscurities, shades, margins, fringes, penumbras, and what James has called "the vague and inarticulate."[29]

In *Essays in Radical Empiricism*, when James replies to the question, "For whom is pure experience 'available'?" his answer is rather strong: "Only new-born babes, or men in semi-coma from sleep, drugs, illnesses, or blows, may be assumed to have an experience pure in the literal sense of a *that* which is not yet any definite *what*, tho' ready to be all sorts of whats."[30] Here we have a second sense of pure experience, as describing the world as it *was*, before consciousness arose. It is important to realize, however, that "pure experience," as a descriptive term for either the present moment or the past, is *itself* a conception, a second-hand experience for James. "Pure experience" cannot be taken to refer exclusively to the past, because in such a formulation novelty would not be real; change would not take place. This position James would find untenable. But what he also realized, though he often did not state it as clearly, is that "pure experience" cannot be exclusively identified with the present—if the present is taken as immediately given—for exactly the same reasons. He verbalizes this by saying that the present *is not present,* that is, is a passing moment, or by saying that the present is an activity. In short, the key to James's different descriptions of "pure experience" here is to remember that experience grows. "Experience itself, taken at large, can grow by its edges. That one moment of it proliferates into the next by transitions which, whether conjunctive or disjunctive, continue the experiential tissue, can not, I contend, be denied."[31]

In this more processive sense of pure experience, consciousness has arisen as a relational transition between various moments, as these have dropped into the past, achieving "objective immortality" through "prehension," to borrow Whitehead's terminology.[32] In a third sense, then, pure experience refers neither exclusively to the present nor to the past, but rather denies that dichotomy as exclusive. "Pure experience" refers to a continuously changing process in which the past enters into the present, and part of the latter's significance is as a positive or negative continuation of the past. In this formulation of pure experience, consciousness arises by way of addition qua relation. But once arisen, it exhibits a curious stubbornness: it cannot simply be reduced to experience again. To do so would be to deny the reality of change. "*The separation of it [pure experience] into consciousness and content comes, not by way of subtraction, but by way of addition*—the addition, to a given concrete piece of it, of other sets of experiences, in connection with which severally its use or function may be of two different kinds."[33]

In this third sense, consciousness has come on the scene, with the result that "it happens relatively seldom that . . . [a] new fact is added *raw*. More usually it is embedded cooked, as one might say, or stewed down in the sauce of the old."[34] On the one hand, pure experience is a continually changing process in which the very relation of consciousness itself *adds* to the reality. This formulation transcends the present/past distinction. On the other hand, consciousness is not all of pure experience, though for grown-ups, as opposed to babes, it would seem that consciousness, or more specifically *language,* is the way toward pure experience. We find ourselves embedded in consciousness, so to speak.

But even this last linguistic formulation of pure experience is a conceptualization, though it refers to a level of reality beneath the exclusivity of concepts. Furthermore, James realized that not only is this "final" conceptualization inadequate, but conceptualization *as such* is inadequate. Nonetheless, conceptualization is necessary. This view is found primarily in *A Pluralistic Universe.*

As we have partially seen in Chapter Two, *A Pluralistic Universe* is written on a religious theme; but it contains ideas absolutely central to the Jamesian notion of pure experience. In *The Principles of Psychology,* James had adopted a dualism. His description of consciousness, however, ultimately rendered his dichotomy inadequate. James began to remedy this in *Essays in Radical Empiricism* by rejecting the consciousness/content dichotomy. He did so by discarding consciousness as a separate substance and retaining only a functional view. But as James continued his specification of the problem, he realized more clearly that not consciousness but *language,* and particularly ideal language, that is, logic, was the "enemy" and had, therefore, to be rejected. He says, in a strong statement, quoted earlier:

> For my own part, I have finally found myself compelled to
> *give up the logic,* fairly, squarely, and irrevocably. It has
> an imperishable use in human life, but that use is not to
> make us theoretically acquainted with the essential nature

of reality. . . . Reality, life, experience, concreteness, immediacy, use what word you will, exceeds our logic, overflows and surrounds it. If you like to employ words eulogistically, as most men do, and so encourage confusion, you may say that reality obeys a higher logic, or enjoys a higher rationality. But I think that even eulogistic words should be used rather to distinguish than to commingle meanings, so I prefer bluntly to call reality if not irrational then at least non-rational in its constitution,—and by reality here I mean reality where things *happen,* all temporal reality without exception. I myself find no good warrant for even suspecting the existence of any reality of a higher denomination than that distributed and strung-along and flowing sort of reality which we finite beings swim in. That is the sort of reality given us, and that is the sort with which logic is so incommensurable.[35]

James realized that logic, or language, ironically enough, was necessary, even though sometimes insulating. The quotation above indicates as much; furthermore, James was quite willing to ascribe a "primarily theoretical function to our intellect"[36] and not condone a simple reductionism. But he believed that the intellect as such could not deal with the whole of reality, though it cannot avoid dealing with "part" of it. "Thought deals thus solely with surfaces. It can name the thickness of reality, but it cannot fathom it, and its insufficiency here is essential and permanent, not temporary."[37]

In this position reality is greater than the conceptual. More important, it is greater than the possibly conceptual. Reality cannot be completely put into thought, or more specifically, into language. Yet language, as James shows by self-example, is necessary to deal with reality. It follows that reality is available only through language, but the language user must transcend the limitations of language, must show the insufficiency of language itself.

Initially, in attempting to renounce his functional dualism,

James had said that pure experience was available only to new-born babes, persons under anaesthesia, and so forth, in short, to persons who were "unconscious." But in *A Pluralistic Universe*, James, having clarified the problem, became more optimistic. Reality is "available" to those who use language in such a way as to transcend language, to those who are not trapped by the bewitchment of language, to those who realize that the word "activity" is not the experience of activity.

> As long as one continues *talking*, intellectualism remains in undisturbed possession of the field. The return to life can't come about by talking. It is an *act*; to make you return to life, I must set an example for your imitation, I must . . . deafen you to talk, or to the importance of talk, by showing you, as Bergson does, that the concepts we talk with are made for the purposes of *practice* and not for purposes of insight. Or I must *point*, point to the mere *that* of life, and you by inner sympathy must fill out the *what* for yourselves.[38]

There are obvious pragmatic overtones to this position. Words are "indicators" or "signs of direction," so to speak. The meaning of an idea is not just its formal significance, but rather what it can do. And most important, there is *more* to language than just its formal significance. Language, when pragmatically used, points beyond itself toward reality, or is the vehicle toward it. In a sense, language is the house of pure experience, somewhat in the same way that, for Heidegger, "language is the house of Being. In its home man dwells. Whoever thinks or creates in words is a guardian of this dwelling."[39]

Sometimes James refers to reality as the "perceptual,"[40] and as we have seen, this is, at best, a bad choice of words. In "The Function of Cognition," he tells us that the treatment of percepts as the only realm of reality is inadequate. "I now treat concepts as a co-ordinate realm."[41] The conceptual, the linguistic, the logical, then, are all necessary for James, but not sufficient. Language is the house of pure experience, but only when language is used to "point beyond itself." This implicitness about language constitutes its pragmatic character, without which all language would degenerate into a form of "vicious intellectualism." For James, pure experience is available through language, but language cannot describe the whole of pure experience. Furthermore, the inability of language to plumb the depths of pure experience must be pointed out, as we all have a tendency to be bewitched by language, to believe that the only meaning is that of formal significance.

So pure experience does seem to remain faithful to the demands set forth by radical empiricism, that is, that "the only things that shall be debatable among philosophers shall be things definable in terms drawn from experience."[42] "Pure experience" is at least partly available through language, though not captured by language. It can be "recovered," but this recovery is never complete. For one thing, pure experience is continuously changing; as such, novelty is real, and hence recovery is partial. James's position is most aptly termed a "radical realism." Reality—pure experience—is not only *not* coextensive with the known; it is not coextensive with the knowable, in the strong conceptual sense of the term.[43] But there are moments when one can use language to transcend the limitations of language and in such a fashion have a glimpse of "pure experience." Most important, for James, these moments seemed to be comparatively numerous. They were not simply the reward of a privileged class of "philosophers." No one group has exclusive access to reality. Remember that in *Pragmatism*, in a similar fashion, James refused to set up any one discipline as constituting the judge of "making a difference." "Common sense is *better* for one sphere of life, science for another, philosophic criticism for a third; but whether either be *truer* absolutely, Heaven only knows."[44] Experience was seen by James as rich enough to be available on many different levels, each affording a partial perspective. "Profusion, not economy, may after all be reality's key-note."[45]

Conclusion

William James remains a philosopher difficult to type exclusively either as a phenomenologist or as a phenomenalist. Consciousness does not form an ultimate ground in his philosophy, even though its description occupies an extremely important place in *The Principles of Psychology*. Even more clearly, James is not a phenomenalist if that outlook defines sense data as primary and views "reality" as a construct built of such data. A review of James's scattered statements on language reveals a two-level approach. On the first level, reality seems simply at odds with language. In other words, when language is taken as having only formal significance, it is inadequate. James also gives hints of a second position, however, where language is used to point beyond itself toward reality. In this second position, language is the conduit toward pure experience. Using these statements on language as a springboard, I have attempted a description, necessarily incomplete, of James's metaphysics. Pure experience is for James partially available through language, but only when language is recognized as insufficient, that is, as directional.

The major tenet of this volume has been that the theme of "vagueness" occupies a central position in the Jamesian corpus. Ultimately, James was to extend his high regard for vagueness found in *The Principles* to the stage where it took on an ontological dimension. Pure experience is vague in the sense that it is beneath the subject/object dichotomy; it is vague in the sense of being available most primordially as activity, as process; it is vague in the sense that conceptualizations of it are retrospective, not immediate; and finally, it is vague in the sense that even James's own description of it is a hypothesis, one in which he has ultimate faith, to be sure, but a hypothesis nonetheless. It is here that a crucial difference, at least of emphasis, arises between James and Heidegger—or at least some interpretations of the latter philosopher. James does insist that his outlook, with its rejection of "vicious intellectualism," constitutes a *possible* interpretation of reality, a "fully co-ordinate hypothesis" acting in opposition to monism.[46] James's metaphysical outlook is more than a heuristic device, as Ayer might claim, but it seems less than Heidegger would accept. For Heidegger, there is a definite distinction between nature and human existence; furthermore, the universal structures of *Dasein* seem to be read out of, rather than projected into, the situation. As Calvin Schrag has noted:

> Heidegger is explicit and unambiguous in his contention that the task of the phenomenologist has to do with the "lifting off" (*Abhebung*) of the structures of existence as they disclose themselves in the phenomena. Here . . . we see Heidegger's phenomenological side with its insistence on scientific description. But this phenomenological side is never successfully coupled with his method of hermeneutical interpretation which arises from his deeply entrenched historical mode of thinking.[47]

For James, at his best, a claim to "read off" the structures of existence would be unacceptable. All descriptions of the reality are partial, including his own. While James did insist that his position made logical sense, that is, was not "meaningless," he was not satisfied with mere logical possibility.[48] Differently stated, a description or, more precisely, alternative descriptions of the situation and their possible outcomes are incomplete, and essentially so. His empirical interpretation of actual possibility required a view of reality as fundamentally vague—though not completely so. Further, it is the opacity of reality that compels a response, and not simply a description, on our part. Ralph Barton Perry has caught this point extremely well. For James, the real world signifies inexhaustible fecundity. The universe is not an order, but that of which every type of order is only a limited aspect. . . . His universe is a universe by virtue of its omitting nothing, by virtue of its indeterminate immensity and complexity, its unanalyzed ingredients, its unplumbed depths, its passage beyond every horizon, and not by virtue of any architecture, or structural delimitation, whether logical, aesthetic, or moral. . . . This reality that overflows all bounds and fills all interstices, providing a perpetual residuum which escapes even the most meticulous analysis and the most comprehensive generalizations—this reality that runs off the palms and slips through the fingers of the most dexterous thought— is a companion notion to that of selectiveness. . . . But selection always implies omission, something excluded as well as something included. . . . The world is a selection in the making, amidst a superabundance of the unselected.[49]

In sum, the descriptive approaches of both phenomenalism and phenomenology leave something out. "Ever not quite" has to be said of these outlooks also.[50] But the "hermeneutical side" of Heidegger highlights the importance of *pointing,* and in that sense itself reveals its own dimension of being "ever not quite." To this extent it is in tune with James's radical realism.

At the very end of *A Pluralistic Universe,* James tells his audience that *"it is high time for the basis of discussion in these questions to be broadened and thickened up."*[51] He saw himself as contributing to this thickening. Reality at its most primordial level appears as a "more" for James, as profusion. It is beyond *completely* objective description, and essentially so. To say the same thing differently, all metaphysical statements involve an element of belief.[52] Reality exceeds logic: "being is . . . attested," to use Gabriel Marcel's excellent phrase.[53] Language, correctly used, can aid in our realizing this. To the end, James remained committed to the belief that human beings can experience more, ontologically, than they can linguistically conceptualize or describe.[54]

If the "interpretation" advanced in the past four chapters is accepted, then the "pragmatic upshot" is somewhat radical. Philosophic systems per se involve partiality, although this is not the same as saying that one is as good as another. Description, although important, gives way to direction, to viewing James's texts as a provocation to "go beyond." Interpretations, or provocations, have consequences, good or bad, in everyday experience.

It is in response to James's invitation that the following two parts of this volume attempt such a "leap," first, by carrying on conversations with other philosophical texts and disclosing their hidden Jamesian dimensions; and second, by trying to go beyond and apply Jamesian texts to concrete situations.

PART TWO

CONVERSATIONS

The pragmatists [e.g., William James] tell us that the conversation which it is our moral duty to continue is merely our project, the European intellectual's form of life. It has no metaphysical nor epistemological guarantee of success. . . . We are not conversing because we have a goal, but because Socratic conversation is an activity which is its own end. . . . The pragmatist must avoid saying, with Peirce, that truth is fated to win. He must even avoid saying that truth will win.

RICHARD RORTY, "Pragmatism, Relativism, and Irrationalism"

The recurring double point of James's pragmatism is that all theory is practice (situated intellectual involvement with real local effects) and that all practices are not equally worthy.

FRANK LENTRICCHIA, *Ariel and the Police*

Chapter Five

James, Peirce, and "The Will to Believe"

The multidimensionality of the term "pragmatism" is a well-known phenomenon. Much has been made of the Peircean pragmatic theory of meaning vis-à-vis the Jamesian pragmatic theory of truth. Sometimes the contrast is made too quickly. This results in the undervaluing of important similarities between the two thinkers.

It has often been said that the Jamesian position appealed to the affective dimension in life, in the sense of our having the "right to believe" in a hypothesis when the situation is unsolvable, yet forced, living, and momentous. Further, James's metaphysics of "pure experience" involves more than just theoretical knowledge. James held the position that the human being is capable of experiencing dimensions of reality not completely reducible to the knowable, in the strong sense of that term. "Pure experience" is not an objective ground that can be demonstrated with certainty. In this sense, Jamesian metaphysics, as we have seen, demands an element of "commitment."

This chapter suggests that these same elements, the affective or the will to believe, also play an important role in Peirce's position. More specifically, as Peirce begins to refine his pragmatic method, he reacts against two things: nominalism and personalism. Both of these have one thing in common: they emphasize the "foreground" of experience. Peirce reacts by emphasizing the "background" of experience. Science is the study of the "useless"; pragmatism defines meaning in terms of conceivable effects "in the long run." The ongoing scientific community becomes the basic unit of reference, and so forth. The two elements of nominalism and personalism are not so easily collapsible, however. In reacting to these two different types of individualism, Peirce sets the stage for the question, What is the relationship between realism and meaning? Differently put, Peirce moved from a narrow to a broad definition of pragmatism. So much is well known. But Peirce's broader definition, which is *not* metaphysically neutral, contains an element of conviction or commitment. The relationship between meaning and realism is actually the relationship between epistemology and metaphysics. How does this relationship function for Peirce? In my opinion, the possibilities are two: if one tries to justify Peirce's metaphysics via his pragmatic epistemology, the latter must be widened still further, to include an affective dimension of preference. If one tries to justify Peirce's epistemology via his metaphysics, here too an element of commitment is involved, insofar as Peirce's entire cosmological outlook is not capable of sustained verification. Let us see how this comes about.

Peirce's pragmatism is developed within the doubt-inquiry-belief-action matrix made famous in the article "How to Make Our Ideas Clear." The Cartesian approach is rejected as insufficient. So is any claim to direct, intuitive knowledge. For Peirce, if two beliefs alleviate the same doubt content by producing the same habit of action, then they are identical. Here is pragmatism being born; "what a thing means is simply what habits it involves."[1] In the well-known example of the meaning of calling something "hard," however, Peirce initially gives a very positivistic description of the situation. "There is absolutely no difference between a hard thing and a soft thing as long as they are not brought to the test." This stance, if consistently maintained, would commit Peirce to strict operational definitions and, furthermore, to nominalism. "Generals" would be viewed as abstractions; disposition terms could not be properly defined. Ultimately, laws in science would be seen as mere duplications of physical phenomena. As such they would be expendable on *pragmatic* grounds as superfluous.[2] The scope of the difficulty becomes more obvious when one applies the pragmatic method to a term like "reality" and asks, What does it mean to say that *x* is real? Peirce defined real things in terms of their effects, which was to cause belief.[3] But he wanted to hold the position that ultimately some shared opinion would come about. Such a position is best stated in terms of the contrary-to-fact conditional, as indeed are the laws of science in general. Peirce, of course, realized all this and later on indicated that pragmatism was *not* to be taken in a neutral positivistic sense: "The question is, not what *did* happen, but whether it would have been well to engage in any line of conduct whose successful issue depended upon whether that diamond *would* resist an attempt to scratch it, or whether all other logical means of determining how it ought to be classed *would* lead to the conclusion which, to quote the very words of the article, would be 'the belief which alone could be the result of the investigation carried *sufficiently far*.'"[4]

This text is important because it clearly indicates Peirce's emphasis on the subjunctive; pragmatism is not neutral; it is to be associated with the metaphysical stance of scholastic realism, which advocates the reality of generals; "possibility is sometimes of a real kind."[5] This broader view of pragmatism avoids the problems of operational definitions,[6] but Peirce's new nonneutral metaphysical position raises the question of whether or not it can be justified by his epistemology.[7]

It is clear that Peirce did not want merely to conflate truth and reality, as in some form of idealism. But it is also clear that he rejected the position wherein reality is completely independent of all thought, forever and ever. For Peirce, such a view would "block the way of inquiry."[8] Rather does Peirce define reality as independent of what you or I or any finite group of people might think about it, but not as necessarily independent of thought in general.[9] Going further, Peirce asserts that the opinion ultimately fated to be agreed on by the community of scientific investigators is what is meant by truth, and the "object represented in this opinion is the real."[10] From this perspective, then, individual beliefs are clearly "constrained"; also present or future opinions held in a communal fashion are subject to constraint at this very moment. Only in the ultimate case limit where a completely shared opinion is arrived at do we have coextension of knowledge and reality. Such a position raises the question, How do we get from here to there? Peirce's reply is normative: we ought to get from here to there by employing the pragmatic method.[11]

But which version? Clearly, the broader of the two definitions is needed. Only by employing a version of the method that allows for the reality of generals can Peirce say that, even now, we are subject to constraint by a reality that exhibits independence in some sense. But can one employ the pragmatic method itself to establish that there is some conceivable difference between nominalism and realism? Can the epistemology be used to justify the metaphysical stance? Arthur Burks, in an insightful introduction to Peirce's thought, argues that it cannot:

> The sole difference between the nominalist's and the realist's conception of law has to do with potentialities; and there can be a genuine dispute between the two only if propositions involving potentialities alone have practical consequences. But clearly they do not. It can make no practical difference to say of a diamond that has not been and never will be tested whether it would or would not have been scratched if it had been tested. So long as we agree to the law "All diamonds are hard" and its practical consequence that "If this diamond *is* tested it will not be scratched," then it can make no practical difference what we hold of a diamond that is *never* tested. An untested diamond is beyond practical interest. Another

way of putting the matter is to say that action is based on actualities, not on potentialities, and that potentialities cannot affect conduct.[12]

In a footnote, Burks goes on to say that we do act on potentialities in the sense that "feelings of regret" are possible. For example, one might regret having made a particular speech, because had I not, I would have won the election. Burks asserts, however, that such feelings of regret are not part of the conceivable effects of a belief. Such effects are "not consequences of the belief itself . . . but rather are consequences of holding the belief,"[13] that is, they are emotional associations of the belief. Now it is undoubtedly true that Peirce often argued in this fashion, namely, against the sentient, the private, the merely satisfying, and so forth, particularly when he was reacting to James's position, which he considered too individualistic and too conduct-oriented. But there also seems to be at least one instance where Peirce cannot make this distinction clearly, namely, the belief by the members of a scientific community that they are slowly and correctly arriving at a shared belief. Peirce held that the members of a (the) scientific community were driven by a "cheerful hope"[14] that their investigations would ultimately terminate in truth, if only they used the correct method, namely, pragmatism. "We all hope that the different scientific inquiries in which we are severally engaged are going ultimately to lead to some definitely established conclusion, which conclusion we endeavor to anticipate in some measure."[15] Pragmatism was seen as the required method—not because it was self-justifying in an apodictic sense, but because it was self-criticizing. The "proof" of the method involves an application of the method itself. And Peirce appealed to the "facticity" of the history of scientific achievement as inductive proof that the method worked. Furthermore, if pragmatism did not actually prove realism once and for all, it was at least compatible with the thesis that "there are real things existing independently of us." The method of pragmatism, taken in the broader sense of implying the reality of generals, was supposed to avoid the possibility that a group of scientific investigators would "fix by convention" what the truth would be, because the method forced the individuals to be constrained by experience, by independent reals. But the argument ultimately rests on the cheerful hope that the scientists will act in the manner described and prescribed by Peirce. There is nothing in the argument that would logically prohibit investigators from deciding to hold some belief as paradigmatic in a Kuhnian sense.[16] Indeed, it is at this level that Peirce's "Popperian" philosophy of science comes to the fore. Peirce believed that the "best hypothesis, in the sense of the one most recommending itself to the inquirer, is the one which can be the most readily refuted if it is false."[17] Whereas confirmation only makes a hypothesis more likely, which is to say more in alignment with our preconceptions, Peirce did believe that hypotheses could be falsified. He had an implicit faith in scientific method as honest, a faith capable of inductive justification, but a faith, nevertheless. Karl Popper argues in the same fashion, admitting that at any given moment "we are prisoners caught in the framework of our theories; our expectations; our past experiences; our language. But we are prisoners in a Pickwickian sense: if we try, we can break out of our framework at any time. Admittedly, we shall find ourselves again in a framework, but it will be a better and roomier one; and we can at any moment break out of it again."[18]

But as Thomas Kuhn has shown so well, if this were so, "there ought to be no very special difficulties about stepping into someone else's framework in order to evaluate it."[19] Kuhn's conclusion is that Popper "has characterized the entire scientific enterprise in terms that apply only to its occasional revolutionary parts,"[20] and further, that when a transfer does take place between paradigms, it is a "conversion experience that cannot be forced."[21] We need not take a position here on the Kuhn-Popper debate. The point is rather that Peirce himself made an act of faith in scientific method. While he believed that "the perversity of thought of whole generations may cause the postponement of the ultimate fixation"[22] of belief, ultimately, he would not accept a Kuhnian analysis. On this he was adamant. Also, the issue here cannot be dealt with merely by pointing to the history of science. It is precisely what that history is that is at issue.

We might sum the discussion up in a negative fashion by saying that Peirce's distinction among the four methods—tenacity, authority, a priori, and scientific[23]—is overdrawn. Peirce himself is tenacious in advocating the scientific method of pragmatism over all others, and he becomes more tenacious as James develops his own position. This does not mean that Peirce could not give good reasons for his position. His reasons were numerous, brilliant, and well-articulated. Positively summarized, however, in the last analysis, Peirce's "cheerful hope" involves a Jamesian "will to believe" in a *situation* that is forced, living, and momentous.

What is the situation? Ultimately, it concerns reality, the known, and the knowable. Peirce was willing to admit that reality is not coextensive with the known, but not that reality was not know*able*. To take such a stance would be, in his opinion, to "block the road to inquiry." James might respond that *only* such a stance (reality as greater than knowable) keeps our theoretical concepts honest. In a vague, unfinished universe, one can avoid self-deception only if one admits the essential tentativeness of all hypotheses. This, on a metatheoretical level, is a stratagem, an attitude, taken on James's part toward reality. Graham Bird sums up the issue as follows: "He [James] took the view that no theory is ever a complete transcript of reality, and that there need be no ultimate or final Truth. Unlike Peirce, who denied the latter view, James expressed serious qualms about that denial. . . . Like Quine James was not prepared simply to accept the ideal of a final unique truth. As in terrestrial travel the horizon is something we may aim at, but there is no hope of finally arriving without some further horizon presenting itself."[24]

Peirce assumes the opposite stratagem to the one adopted by James, although he notes that "in practice" they may come to the same thing.[25] For him, it is "better" to assume the stance or hope that reality is knowable—at least that this is possible. But this stance is a Peircean "will to believe." Furthermore, part of the meaning of adopting it *is* the consequences of holding it, on the part of the members of the scientific community. The "cheerful hope" cannot be expressed solely in terms of conceivable effects that would occur. Part of the "meaning" of the cheerful hope is its function as a catalyst. Otherwise, an infinite regress is the result.

What, then, has this to do with the possibility of justifying Peirce's metaphysics in terms of his epistemology? Simply this: if one tries to make the distinction between nominalism and realism simply in terms of conceivable effects, that is, *meaning,* such a distinction can be made if pragmatism is broadened still further, if the affective dimension is included, or better, if, at least in some instances, the "consequences of belief" versus "consequences of holding that belief" dichotomy is rejected. To do so flies in the teeth of Peirce's admitted emphasis on the conceptual vis-à-vis the affective. But at a metatheoretical level, Peirce seems to have no other choice. He chooses a different "belief" than James, but his choice is made ultimately in the same way. In short, Peirce's pragmatic epistemology can make room for or justify his metaphysical realism only if it is admitted that an extralogical dimension is involved.

But this is only half the question. If Peirce's epistemology cannot justify his metaphysics without a "belief factor," can his metaphysics justify his epistemology without one? Here the issue is more obvious, and we can be briefer. The outcome is the same, however: an extralogical dimension is involved.

Metaphysically, Peirce developed an objective idealism, to account for his "realist" approach to laws in science. Mind is viewed as basic and as capable of associating, of taking on habits. "Ideas tend to spread continuously and to affect certain others which stand to them in a peculiar relation of affectability."[26] The habits are the laws of nature. Matter from this perspective is viewed as frozen mind, as hidebound. Peirce viewed the universe as containing both a tychistic dimension and an anancastic aspect. But neither of these was a sufficient explanation of how things evolve. Peirce's evolutionary cosmology is "agapastic." The universe is moving from chance toward order, though at any given moment one can find aspects of both. Habits tend to spread and connect with others, in accordance with Peirce's principle of "synechism." Finally, the universe is viewed as "a vast representamen, a great symbol of God's purpose, working out its conclusions in living realities."[27] Such an outlook is remarkable for its richness and detail, yet it clearly involves an extralogical dimension. Peirce himself viewed metaphysical outlooks as "guesses" based on current scientific facts. But his own exposition is clearly anthropomorphic. While Peirce, indeed, would have been the first to admit this,[28] it does raise questions about the self-sufficiency of a metaphysical position. But there is a bigger problem: Peirce asserted that his evolutionary outlook "constitutes a hypothesis capable of being tested by experiment."[29] Yet it is highly questionable whether the thesis that we are moving from firstness through thirdness toward secondness in accordance with the principle of cosmic love constitutes a verifiable or, better, falsifiable proposition—or ever could do so. Peirce espoused a belief in God and advocated reverie as a "base" (i.e., the "humble argument") that might be partially justified by the more logical "neglected argument." But as he himself held, the base is "abductive," and there is no complete logic of abduction. Finally, Peirce's agapastic evolutionary position is vehemently opposed to the "gospel of greed" and is, in his words, his "own passionate predilection. . . . Yet the strong feeling is in itself, I think, an argument of some weight in favor of the agapastic theory of evolution,—so far as it may be presumed to bespeak the normal judgment of the Sensible Heart."[30] Such references to feeling and the sensible heart seem clearly to indicate that at least aspects of Peirce's metaphysical cosmology are value-laden. To be sure, Peirce's contribution here is not a small one. But on this level also, an element of "conviction" or "commitment" is involved.

Conclusion

The predominant approach to Peirce is to divorce his epistemology and his metaphysics, or at least his cosmology. The latter is "generally regarded by contemporary philosophers as the black sheep or white elephant of his philosophical progeny."[31] By way of contrast, in his insightful book *Purpose and Thought: The Meaning of Pragmatism*, John Smith has argued against any such dichotomy. "The theory of science and of truth cannot, in Peirce's view, be elaborated without reference to a larger context embracing the nature of the real and its relation to the inquirer who seeks to grasp it in the form of truth."[32] In this sense, for Smith, the very success of science must be viewed in a larger context, one of ontological dimensions. The achievements of "scientific inquiry are not left in their immediacy at the level of brute fact but must be understood as manifestations of patterns of development underlying the evolution of the entire universe."[33] One purpose of this chapter has been to indicate, in one way, why Smith's "holistic" approach is more adequate.[34] Specifically, the distinction between Peirce's epistemology and his metaphysics is often made in terms of the logical versus the psychological, the objective versus the subjective. I have shown that it is a mistake to employ this distinction, because on *both* the level of epistemology and that of a metaphysical cosmology, a so-called psychological element, a belief factor, is involved. In reacting to nominalism and personalism—both "foreground" experiences—Peirce underestimates important differences between the two. In arguing against nominalism and for realism, Peirce espouses a position wherein *actual* possibility exists. But in reacting against the personal, the affective, and so forth, Peirce argues for the meaningful and ultimately advocates a position wherein possibility can exist only as logical possibility— as *possible* possibility. This ultimately sets up the question of the relation of Peirce's theory of meaning to his theory of reality. In a sense, Peirce's theory of meaning evolves into a theory of truth, since it points toward a reality that is not completely "meaning-ful." In sum, whether one grounds Peirce's metaphysics in his epistemology or his epistemology in his metaphysics, a version of James's "will to believe" seems to be a necessary ingredient.

Chapter Six

Text, *Con*text, and the Existential Limit: "The Will to Believe" in Dewey and Marx

Karl-Otto Apel, in his book *Charles Sanders Peirce, From Pragmatism to Pragmaticism*, opens with the following comment: "Despite the exaggeration and simplification that is involved in the revelation of any complex truth, it can be said that in the world of so-called industrial society there are exactly three philosophies that really function. By this I do not mean just that they are advocated, but that they in fact mediate between theory and practice in life. These philosophies are Marxism, Existentialism and Pragmatism." [1] Furthermore, Apel specifically sees James's pragmatic contribution as involving an existentialist dimension. "In his essay *The Will to Believe*, William James introduced Kierkegaard's central concern—the individual's subjective interest in fundamentally unprovable and therefore existentially relevant truth—into the context of the community of scientific experimenters, proposing such truth as the limit of this community." [2] Apel's emphasis on the existential dimension in James surfaces most clearly in two of James's essays, "The Sentiment of Rationality" and "The Will to Believe." In the former, James argues that we do not select one ultimate hypothesis over another for merely rational reasons. Conceptualizations of life are partial, and even if we had a complete nonperspectival outlook, the human being would continue to question, to point at the void beyond. We recall that, for James, the bottom of being or reality is "logically opaque"[3] to us. In such a situation, he argues, we will select one hypothesis over another in terms of its sentimental appeal. We will not accept an outlook that is ultimately pessimistic or one that gives us no set role to play. "Pretend what we may, the whole man within us is at work when we form our philosophical opinions. Intellect, will, taste, and passion co-operate just as they do in practical affairs."[4]

This position is extended in his 1896 article "The Will to Believe," where James argues that there are certain situations that are "forced, living, and momentous," and where one must make a decision partially on passional grounds. *"Our passional nature not only lawfully may, but must, decide an option between propositions, whenever it is a genuine option that cannot by its nature be decided on intellectual grounds."*[5] This position has often been misinterpreted as a plea for mere subjectivism, as a thesis that we can believe whatever makes us feel good. But James clearly argues against such an outlook. For example, we cannot simply believe that we are well and about while lying in bed overpowered by rheumatism; we cannot feel sure that the two dollars in our pocket are one hundred dollars, and so forth. The reason for this is that the will to believe is operative only in those situations where one has two diverse hypotheses, each equally coherent and each capable of corresponding to empirical data to an equal extent. What James is not so clear about is whether there are any hypotheses whose content by definition precludes them from being forced, living, and momentous, and requiring the will to believe. A seemingly obvious candidate would be hypotheses in science. (We shall see the importance of this issue for Dewey and Marx later on.) Actually, James is at his best when he does not exclude any hypothesis by definition from the will-to-believe domain, and this chapter argues that the will to believe becomes operative at a crucial stage in the philosophy both of Marx and of Dewey, though neither is clearly aware of it. In this sense, a reconstruction of these philosophic positions shows each to be more Jamesian than either would have thought, and in addition, shows James's influence in areas such as the limits of the social and political— areas that he perhaps did not fully intend to influence.

Dewey

John Dewey is clearly an antifoundationalist philosopher, one for whom philosophy reflects and perfects via critical analyses the concerns and values of a specific community. "The distinctive office, problems and subjectmatter of philosophy grow out of stresses and strains in the community life in which a given form of philosophy arises, and . . . accordingly, its specific problems vary with the changes in human life that are always going on and that at times constitute a crisis and a turning point in human history."[6]

From this perspective, it follows that there is no such an entity as a completely noncontextual philosophy. Indeed, the attempt to find such an outlook is actually an attempt to find certainty. Such an outlook would transcend all contexts and as such as would be relevant to none. Rather, Dewey says, when "context is taken into account, it is seen that every generalization occurs under limiting conditions set by the contextual situation."[7] Certainty must be rejected as a quest, for it fosters several false dualisms. The most important of these is the subject/object dichotomy, often found as the debate between traditional idealism and materialism; this dualism results in the ripping of an organism out of its specific environmental context, so as to see it as an impartial spectator, viewing experience or being in a detached, objective fashion. Philosophy, when it views such an outlook as optimal, is advocating the rejection of context. It leads to an unacceptable (because noncontextual) position where true human progress is no longer possible, or differently stated, it leads to a simple repetition of the past, of the past of philosophy with a capital *P* (in Richard Rorty's sense of the term),[8] and not to a confrontation with and idealization of the best aspects of the present situation. From this, philosophy needs to be saved or recovered. As Dewey put it, "Philosophy recovers itself when it ceases to be a device for dealing with the problems of philosophers and becomes a method, cultivated by philosophers, for dealing with the problems of men."[9] And again, "I believe that philosophy in America will be lost between chewing a historic cud long since reduced to woody fiber, or an apologetics for lost causes (lost to natural science), or a scholastic, schematic formalism, unless it can somehow bring to consciousness America's own needs and its own implicit principle of successful action."[10]

But what method was it that Dewey advocated to accomplish such a task, or set of tasks? In a contextualist philosophy, a method must be employed that can deal with change and novelty, a method that identifies inquiry with discovery of the new rather than with exclusive repetition of the old. Such a method, Dewey argued, can be found in the development of modern science, and he advocated that the *form* of scientific methodology, as opposed to any specific content, serve as a model. The scientific method, whose origin began with Francis Bacon's realization that knowledge is power, has, for Dewey, the following characteristics.[11] First, it is future- rather than past-oriented. Ideas, qua hypotheses, are to be tried out, not received uncritically. Second, the method advocates the interpenetration of thought and action. To have an idea is insufficient; one must act on it in the "laboratory." Third, it was communal or cooperative. Individuals, left to themselves, will simply repeat the experiments of other scientists, or worse, fall into self-deception. Finally, the method was self-corrective. It did not advocate certainty, but rather recognized the novel and the precarious. The method "learns from failures as from successes." As late as 1948 Dewey wrote, in the second introduction to *Reconstruction in Philosophy:* "Here, then, lies the reconstructive work to be done by philosophy. It must undertake to do for the development of inquiry into human affairs and hence into morals what philosophers of the last few centuries did for promotion of scientific inquiry in physical and physiological conditions and aspects of human life." [12]

Now a first criticism of such a suggestion from a Marxist (or indeed other) perspective might well be that it ignores fundamental differences between the natural and the social or human. That is, Dewey's emphasis on interaction and transaction between organism and environment downplays the class structure and ignores the social nature that is constituted by a person's labor, by the creation of his or her species-being through praxis.

Dewey might be able to respond, however, at least partially, to such criticism, indicating that all he wished to apply was the *form* of scientific method and not any specific content. Indeed, to do otherwise would be to lapse into a neglect of specifying contextual dimensions. But, what the critique begins to point up is a serious criticism of Dewey, which can be developed in several ways. For the sake of brevity, I will limit discussion to two versions. First, the form/content distinction is itself one of those dualisms that Dewey over and over again renounces. In *Art as Experience*, for example, he specifically renounces a disjunctive analysis of works of art from either an exclusively formal or an exclusively content-wise perspective. Indeed, he tells the reader that "the truth of the matter is that what is form in one connection is matter in another and vice-versa. Color that is matter with respect to expressiveness of some qualities and values is form when it is used to convey delicacy, brilliance, gayety." [13] A second way of making this point might be to suggest that Dewey's analysis of science is not actually how science proceeds, but is rather a formal idealization. What is at issue here is the very meaning of the terms "science" and "scientific method," and whether that method can be separated from its specific social and historical context.

It must be noted that Dewey himself, at times, seems well aware of this. In "The Pattern of Inquiry," for example, Dewey gives what is perhaps the most detailed description of his method: indeterminate situations become "problematic" through the use of inquiry, that is, they become more determinate insofar as we crystallize what has gone wrong specifically and then hypothe-size what to do about it. "*Inquiry is the controlled or directed transformation of an indeterminate situation into one that is so determinate in its constituent distinctions and relations as to con-vert the elements of the original situation into a unified whole.*" [14] But here Dewey is careful to say that logical forms of inquiry are not transcendental; "formal conceptions arise out of . . . ordinary transactions; they are not imposed upon them from on high or from any external and *a priori* source. But when they are formed they are also *formative;* they regulate the proper conduct of the activities out of which they develop." [15] And again, "The way in which men *do* 'think' denotes, as it is *here* interpreted, simply the ways in which men at a given time carry on their inquiries. So far as it is used to register a difference from the ways in which they *ought* to think, it denotes a difference like that between good and bad farming or good and bad medical practice." [16]

Here the form of the scientific method does not seem to sepa-rate completely from specific content, and indeed, it is conceivable that it might possibly be abandoned. Nevertheless, the form of the scientific method, as envisioned by Dewey, has had success and is, on that basis, powerful, that is, itself informing. As John Smith has put it, in Dewey's view, "logical forms which have proved them-selves effective *up to a given time* can be regarded as *a priori* with regard to the inquiry at hand." [17] Dewey sees scientific method as incremental, as adding on relational properties to the world of commonsense experience (not substituting for the latter). To quote Smith again, for Dewey, "scientific inquiry necessarily in-volves the *transformation* of familiar commonsense objects with their immediate cultural qualities and associations into scientific objects which are shorn of these associations and are meant to have universal import. . . . [A]n *increment of meaning* accrues to things when they are seen in the context of scientific inquiry." [18]

In short, the form of the scientific method is one of compara-tive intellectual disinterestedness, and Dewey seemed to believe, and to be able to give some reasons warranting the belief, that the use of this method could enable people to go from the relatively particular (specific cultural situation) to the comparatively universal (what specific situations have in common). Such a position is defensible, but it does presuppose a Jamesian belief factor. Consider, for contrast effect, the view of science proposed by Thomas Kuhn, in his text *The Structure of Scientific Revolutions.* For Kuhn, what one calls "true" or "false" or even "meaningful" in science is determined by the already accepted paradigm of a given "normal science." Normal science is science based on an assumed "paradigm"—a word used frequently and not univocally by Kuhn.[19] A paradigm is a model or standard illustration of scientific achievement that includes law, theory, application, and instrumentation together and is more "basic" than any of these.[20] Normal science is cumulative because progress is defined in terms of the already assumed paradigm. Revolutionary science describes the type of activity that occurs as we move from one paradigm to another. Such movement is cataclysmic. We leap holistically from one framework to another by a process not capable of complete rational explanation. In some sense, a conversion experience is involved.[21] In other words, there is no meaning invariance (e.g., in terms of a common observation language, or a scientific method) that endures in the transition from one method to another.

Now my purpose here is not to defend Kuhn's position wholeheartedly, but rather to use his view as a foil to highlight Dewey's assumptions about science. In the end, Dewey had, I believe, great *faith* in the scientific method. He took over a position originated by Peirce that the method of science was superior to other methods, such as tenacity, authority, and the a priori, and adopted Peirce's view that the members of a scientific community are united by a "cheerful hope" that some opinion is ultimately fated to be agreed on in an open way by those who practice the method of science.[22] Dewey differed from Peirce in consciously applying the scientific method not only to areas of natural science, but to areas of social concern, to the realms of politics and morals. In other words, Dewey advocated a position where a truly democratic approach to human issues could take place only by applying the scientific method, and he believed that applying that method would ultimately lead to progress.

Such an outlook, while laudable in its tolerance, does not confront the possibility that, in certain situations, one person or society might be confronted with two theoretical accounts of an issue, equally coherent and corresponding equally well to empirical facts, where a decision nonetheless had to be made. Such a position, albeit on a personal level, is precisely what James had in mind in "The Will to Believe." In such a situation the issue is forced, living, and momentous.

Indeed, one might bring out the Jamesian element here by comparing Kuhn's view of science with Dewey's; both positions are coherent, that is, "meaningful"; both can employ empirical evidence to which the theories will correspond. To reconstruct Dewey in this fashion for comparative purposes is, of course, unfair to Dewey, who preceded Kuhn. But it does serve to point up the fact that Dewey, at times, was overoptimistic about at least the form of what he called the "scientific method." Or differently stated, he exercised the will to believe, consciously or unconsciously, or quasi-consciously.

Marx

Karl Marx, no less than John Dewey, was dissatisfied with a view of philosophy as foundational, as merely reflecting or copying a preexistent and static reality. This is elliptically apparent in his oft-quoted statement that "the philosophers have only *interpreted* the world, in various ways; the point, however, is to *change* it." [23] But the contextualism of philosophy is even more clearly stated in an 1842 newspaper article on press censorship. Marx says: "Philosophers do not grow like mushrooms, out of the earth; they are the outgrowth of their period, their nation, whose most subtle, delicate and invisible juices abound in the philosophical ideas. The same spirit that constructs the philosophical system in the mind of the philosopher builds the railways with the hands of the trade. Philosophy does not reside outside this world just as the mind does not reside outside man just because it is not located in his belly." [24] Commenting on this text, Shlomo Avineri notes that it has an implicit critical dimension: "Philosophy is always related to historical actuality, but the philosophical medium itself sometimes severs the link between reality and its philosophical reflection. This, according to Marx, may cause the illusion that the object of philosophy is philosophy itself. A merely contemplative attitude, according to Marx, contains its objects in its contemplation and is thus object-less." [25] Philosophy nonetheless has at least a necessary role to play, for it is only as an adequate interpretation of the world evolves that change is possible. Avineri continues: "In Marx's opinion, theory must evolve an adequate interpretation of the world before it will be able to change it. The history of philosophy is the continuous search for such an adequate picture of the world. Once such a picture has been formed, it dialectically abolishes itself as a reflection of reality and begins to determine the shaping of a new reality." [26]

Note that the important assumption here concerns whether or not an "adequate" picture can always be completely formed, that is, whether "adequate" means "complete." I argue that it does not. This is the basic point of my comparison between Dewey and Marx, and one to which I will shortly return.

Marx was dissatisfied with both traditional naturalism and its idealistic alternative. This represented for him simply a false dichotomy.

> The chief defect of all hitherto existing materialism—that of Feuerbach included—is that the thing [*Gegenstand*], reality, sensuousness, is conceived only in the form of the *object* [*Objekt*] or of *contemplation* [*Anschauung*], but not as *human sensuous activity, practice,* not subjec-

tively. Hence it happened that the *active* side, in contradistinction to materialism, was developed by idealism—but only abstractly, since of course, idealism does not know real, sensuous activity as such.[27]

In place of such a false bifurcation, Marx wished to put a more holistic account, which might be termed either an idealistic naturalism or a naturalistic idealism. Arguments for both versions have been made, and pragmatically, they may well amount to a matter of emphasis. What is more clear is that the extreme formulation of either position results in too much of a reductionism. An overly naturalistic account of Marx's philosophy results in some form of "vulgar Marxism," that is, in a view where the active role of the subject is extremely diminished, if not obliterated. It must be said that Marx himself is at least unintentionally responsible for this overly naturalistic account. In the preface to *A Contribution to the Critique of Political Economy*, for example, Marx takes up the question of legal relationships and regards these as not self-sustaining or self-understandable; rather, "they are rooted in the material conditions of life." [28] In this they are typical of a whole series of disciplines, including politics and philosophy, that emerges as part of the superstructure, which is built on an economic "base." As Marx put it:

> In the social production which men carry on they enter into definite relations that are indispensable and independent of their will; these relations of production correspond to a definite state of development of their material powers of production. The sum total of these relations of production constitutes the economic structure of society—the real foundation, on which rise legal and political superstructures and to which correspond definite forms of social consciousness. The mode of production in material life determines the general character of the social, political, and spiritual processes of life. It is not the con-

sciousness of men that determines their existence, but, on the contrary, their social existence determines their consciousness.[29]

Overemphasis on texts such as this one ignores the idealist dimension of Marx's philosophy and downplays the view of human beings as creating their own species-being through labor, through praxis. As one commentator has put it:

> The origins of Marx's epistemology . . . are deeply imbedded in the German idealist tradition. . . . According to Marx, nature cannot be discussed as if it were severed from human action, for nature as a potential object for human cognition has already been affected by previous human action or contact. Hence nature is never an opaque datum. The phrases "humanized nature" and "humanism equals naturalism" recur in Marx's writings, and "naturalism" in his sense is virtually the opposite of what is generally implied by this term in traditional philosophical discussion. . . . The identification of human consciousness with the practical process of reality as shaped by man is Marx's epistemological and historiosophical achievement.[30]

Such an outlook clearly restores the activity dimension to Marx's philosophy and clearly gives the human self (qua social animal) *an,* and perhaps even *the,* essential role to play. But an interesting irony occurs at just this juncture. Avineri admits that Marx's outlook is different from that of Hegel in the sense that "the constructive nature of human consciousness cannot be limited to merely cognitive action. He [Marx] views cognitive action as the whole process of the development and evolution of reality: getting acquainted with reality constitutes shaping and changing it."[31] From such a perspective the self shapes nature, and his or her being is in turn shaped by it. "Where Feuerbach naturalizes man," Avineri argues, "Marx humanizes nature."[32] Such a view is not reductive in that it does not result in a static foundational rationalism. Taken in a wider sense, however, it is reductive to the extent that nature always appears as meaningful. Avineri is explicit on this, saying above that human nature is never an opaque datum and even going on to draw an explicit contrast between Marx (for Avineri, at least) and William James:

> Whereas pragmatism starts with the premise that man adapts himself to a given, pre-existing environment, Marx views man as shaping his world. Marx's views are also quite incompatible with William James' other premise about the basic irrationality of the external world. Marx, on the contrary, always argues that the world is open to rational cognition because it is ultimately shaped by man himself and man can reach an adequate understanding of his historical activity.[33]

Such a contrast is overdrawn, at least. True, the pragmatists, or at least James and Dewey, are realists in the sense that one always has to conform to an external reality. To assume otherwise would be, for James, to engage in "vicious intellectualism."[34] But note that, in *Experience and Nature*, Dewey, while arguing against the alleged all-inclusiveness of cognitive experience, nonetheless also argues against the definition in advance of any experience as unavailable to human cognition: "It is not denied that any experienced subject-matter whatever may *become* an object of reflection and cognitive inspection. But the emphasis is upon 'become'; the cognitive never *is* all-inclusive: that is, when the material of a prior non-cognitive experience is the object of knowledge, it and the act of knowing are themselves included within a new and wider non-cognitive experience—and *this* situation can never be transcended."[35] Stated differently, reality is malleable, continuously changing, a quasi-chaos, in Jamesian terms.[36] We could not simply conform to it even if we wanted to. Moreover, all attempts to interpret reality themselves become part of reality, as James noted in developing his metaphysics. "Experience itself, taken at large, can grow by its edges."[37] In one sense, then, the connection between pragmatism (James and Dewey) and Marx is much closer than Avineri would allow for.

But there is a second perspective from which Avineri himself at times seems to realize that this contrast is overdrawn. That is, having offered an idealistic and rather rationalistic account of Marx's epistemology and metaphysics, he then notes that this account is inapplicable because of existing social-political conditions.

> Marx's epistemology occupies a middle position between classical materialism and classical idealism. Historically it draws on both traditions; and, since it synthesizes the two traditions, it transcends the classic dichotomy between subject and object. Indirectly this synthesis solves the Kantian antimony between the cognitive and the moral spheres. But Marx thinks that present circumstances still make it impossible to practice this new, adequate epistemology: alienation indicates the continuing existence of the dichotomy between subject and object, as a result of the still distorted process of cognition.
>
> Marx's epistemology thus conceals an internal tension. It tries to solve the traditional epistemological problems, but it tacitly holds that human consciousness could operate according to the new epistemology only if the obstacles in its way in present society were eliminated.[38]

This statement, though somewhat underplayed in the text, is of crucial importance. What it seems to assert can be put best in terms of a contrary-to-fact conditional: this is what would work best epistemically if we were able to employ it, which by definition we are not. In such an outlook, metaphysically speaking, reality is not presently coextensive with the known, but it is coextensive with the know*able*, that is, with what will ultimately come about. In this respect the outlook is identical with Peirce's belief, shared by Dewey, that some opinion is ultimately fated to be agreed on, given world enough and time. Two crucial questions remain unanswered, however.

First, how do we get from here to there; and second, why does the situation of alienation exist? Marx's response to these questions is, on the surface at least, well known. We are alienated because of capitalist modes of production and the relations of production derived therefrom, and we get from here to there by championing the cause of one specific class, namely, the proletariat, that is, by being consciously partisan. Several commentators have found Marx's description of the causes of alienation unsatisfying, however. Thus Tom Goff, for example, in his book *Marx and Mead: Contributions to a Sociology of Knowledge*, applauds Marx's portrayal of the "authentic existence and essence of man in terms of the idea of praxis. The natural and authentic problematic of human life is . . . social man's interaction with and humanizing of nature; his historical transformation of nature (and therefore of himself as a part of nature) which is both a sustainment of life and its constant development. . . . Man is basically a problem-solver in this sense." [39] But in Goff's opinion, there is something very problematic here and it concerns the human being's propensity for alienation, the tendency to succumb to a particularly historical moment of praxis.

> Marx tends simply to *state* the position on alienation, and then moves directly to specific critiques. He fails to conceptualize, at least not with any clarity, the process and appearance of alienation itself. Without such clarification, it would appear that there is a basic contradiction or at least an incompleteness in the critical perspective. On the one hand, Marx presumes the nature of human reality as an on-going, continuous process of change in respect to dialectically related material products, social forms, ideas

and values. On the other hand, this process is apparently *not* continuous; the problematic of alienation intervenes. But why does this occur? What is the connection between praxis and alienation that would explain the latter, and to what degree does alienation deny praxis? If praxis is a continuous process in which "men set themselves only such problems as they can solve," then what is the basis in praxis itself, for the emergence of this problematic?

In so far as these questions are not answered in Marx's own work, it could be argued that the concept of alienation, as a problematic specific to human life, is simply an *ad hoc* or residual category, tacked on to, yet logically inconsistent with, the theory of praxis. Alienation could be considered an idea that is inconsistent with the "utopian" flavor of the idea of continuous development, yet none the less an idea that is necessary in order to account for the historical experience of discontinuity and tension in human history.[40]

Goff admits that the tension here can be reduced by emphasizing the material or mechanistic aspect of praxis, but such a view diminishes consciousness to a mere epiphenomenon; in short, it approaches a vulgar Marxism. Alienation is seen as caused by natural factors, and it will disappear as these factors themselves evolve in accordance with impersonal laws of economic development. If this option is not selected, however, and if one is not persuaded that there are two completely different versions of Marx, early and late, one is left with the conclusion that Marx's theory is less idealistic than Avineri asserts, and certainly with the feeling that reality is somewhat opaque for both Marx and James. Differently stated, at a critical point in his thinking, Marx chose to exercise James's "will to believe." Unlike Dewey, Marx chose to believe not in a particular method, but rather in a particular class, namely, the proletariat.

In moving from philosophy to the proletariat, Marx moved

from form to content, not unlike Dewey's move regarding the scientific method—but Dewey tried to move from content to form.[41] Both moves are "illegitimate," that is, not completely self-justifying. Dewey seems at times to have seen this and at times not to have. It is not clear whether Marx saw it, but certainly the issue surfaces in the continual debate between critical Marxists and scientific Marxists, that is, between those Marxists who are more voluntarist, more willing to take a chance, more suspicious of "objective" science, and those who see Marx's main contribution as a scientific socialism, a description of the inevitable progress of economic history.[42]

This chapter, or better, this "conversation," has not argued explicitly against the views of either Dewey or Marx. Rather, it indicates one issue on which they overlap, a specifically Jamesian issue, and one of which neither philosopher was totally aware. Specifically, that issue concerns situations where one has to make decisions, before all the evidence is in. One can marshal evidence, both in terms of correspondence and in terms of cohesiveness, for alternative theories. This occurs for Dewey on the issue of method and for Marx on the issue of class. Or rather, it *should* occur. A reconstructed view of Marx and of Dewey shows that there are not available completely objective reasons for their choice of either a specific method or a specific class. There are, rather, conflicting opinions where a forced, living, and momentous decision has to be made. Dewey, to an extent, avoids such a confrontation by espousing too great a faith in the scientific method. He seemed sincerely to believe that social and political issues could and should be solved via this method. Marx, at least to an equal extent, avoids the issue by placing ultimate faith in a particular class and by not allowing the issue to come up. One is to remain partisan and to reject skeptical issues—such as those fostered by situations where the will to believe is required—as merely contemplative and not truly practical. Hazarding a generalization, we might state that it would seem that any nonfoundationalist philosophy or any contextualist position demands, at some level, a

Jamesian will to believe.[43] There is nothing wrong with such a commitment, so long as it is recognized and reasons are given for it. Refusal to admit this results in the pretense that one really has a foundationalist position or in an omission of the reasons why an overt belief or commitment has been made.

Epilogue: Text versus *Con*text

Thus far it has been argued that any nonfoundationalist philosophy, or any contextualist position, seems to demand, at some level, a Jamesian will to believe. One necessary ingredient in James's position, and therefore also in the reconstructed philosophies of Dewey and Marx, is an existential "spirit of seriousness." Admittedly, when certainty or foundationalism is rejected, there is a sense in which "play," that is, the active participation of the organism or class, becomes important. But, and the "but" is important, *all* is not play.

Most recently, the spirit of seriousness has come under attack by the French philosopher Jacques Derrida, who has argued that writing itself prevents us from the possibility of having any metaphysics of presence, that is, of attaining certainty. Derrida asserts his "position" vigorously in the following text:

> Turned towards the lost or impossible presence of the absent origin, this structuralist [or logocentric] thematic of broken immediacy is therefore the saddened, *negative,* nostalgic, guilty, Rousseauistic side of the thinking of play whose other side would be the Nietzschean *affirmation,* that is the joyous affirmation of the play of the world and of the innocence of becoming, the affirmation of a world of signs without fault, without truth, and without origin which is offered to an active interpretation. *This affirmation then determines the noncenter otherwise than as loss of the center.* And it plays without security.[44]

For Derrida, writing, not speech, is primary. *"There is nothing outside of the text."*[45] Further, writing always leaves something (no*thing*) out, condemning us to eternal incompleteness, leaving only a "trace." "Writing is one of the representatives of the trace in general, it is not the trace itself. *The trace itself does not exist.* (To exist is to be, to be an entity, a being-present, *to on*)."[46] And again: "The trace is not a presence but is rather the similacrum of a presence that dislocates, displaces, and refers beyond itself. The trace has, properly speaking, no place, for effacement belongs to the very structure of the trace."[47] While these last two texts might be read to contain an echo of the "ineffable," at least one commentator, Richard Rorty, holds that, in developing his notion of "différance," Derrida adopts a much more radical position than this. *"Différance,"* Rorty tell us, "unlike *trace,* has no more to do with signs than it does with things or gods or minds or any of the other things for which Kantian philosophy has sought the unconditioned conditions."[48] What, then, does Derrida mean by the neologism "différance"? One commentator says the following:

> By differance . . . he [Derrida] means a combined movement of deferment in time and differentiation or distinction in space or in kind. . . .
>
> Differance is thus more "primordial" than the substance or presence of each element in the series or structure. The apparent self-identity of each element is an effect of its difference from and deferral of other elements, none of which has an identity of its own outside the "play" of differential relations. . . . To be at all, each thing must be constituted so it escapes the traditional metaphysical category of being, if being is, as it always is, according to Derrida, defined as a form of presence. Differance can never be present, even though it constitutes presence.[49]

Michael Ryan, from whose work *Marxism and Deconstruction* this description of différance is taken, believes that there are important lessons that these two schools of thought can learn from each other—if Marxism is not taken in the narrow "scientific" sense and deconstruction is not perceived as merely literary criticism. What are the implications of the deconstructionist themes described above for Marxism? In Ryan's analysis, "the implication of undecidability for Marxism is that the formal axioms of scientific Marxism—that revolutionary change is necessarily a result of developing productive forces, that dialectical materialism is *the* way of understanding the world, and so on—are necessarily, like any such system, incomplete." [50] It is in the Marx of the *Grundrisse* that the similarity to Derrida is most apparent, especially regarding relation, difference, and antagonism. "Marx admits that a category like 'production in general,' which seems to reduce difference to identity, is a 'rational abstraction' that fixes a 'common element' that nonetheless is 'itself segmented many times over and splits into [*Auseinanderfahrendes*] different determinations.' " [51] And again (here Ryan quotes Marx), the "categories of bourgeois economics possess a truth for all other forms of society . . . but always with an essential difference [*Unterschied*]." [52] It is Marx's notion of "essential difference," Ryan argues, that rejects any attempt at a final picturing of the world:

> Marx's description of the double act of elevating production to an eternal truth and of debasing distribution by relegating it to history is in its form very similar to Derrida's description of the initiating metaphysical act of elevating consciousness, ideal meaning, self-presence in the mind, and therefore speech to an eternal truth, and of simultaneously debasing spatialization, history, social institutionality, and therefore writing through banishment to an outside. [53]

As a final example, in a deconstructive reading of Marx's *Capital, Volume One*, Ryan argues that Marx "disallows the categorical binary opposition between economic development and political force and that the two, rather than being homogeneous instances that 'interact,' are constituted as an undecidable limit or differential relation of force that cannot be described as an ontology of interactive, yet distinct things or homogeneous entities. Each one is the other, undecidedly."[54] Attempts, therefore, to isolate a concept like "economic development" from "political force" are as inadequate as attempts to isolate "productive forces" from "productive relations." Once again, the attack on "scientific" Marxism is evident. Indeed, viewed deconstructively, scientific Marxism, by advocating the distinction between economics and politics, legitimates "a division of labor that preserves the coercive work form."[55]

There is much in all of this that agrees with and further substantiates the anti-foundationalism of Marx. It is significant, however, that, in the very last sentence of the text, Ryan apologizes for giving "short shrift" to Sartre in the third chapter and suggests that the latter's critique of orthodox Marxism is quite similar to his own approach.[56] Deconstruction has indeed been criticized for leading to a reactionary nonactivist relativism, and Ryan several times argues against such an interpretation; "a possible plurality of truth descriptions does not imply a liberal pluralist vision of the equal validity of all political positions."[57] And again, only "from the viewpoint of capitalist rationalism or party patriarchalism does the persistent positing of an alternative, of a continuous displacement along a seriality of revolutions which is multisectorial and without conclusion, seem 'irrational' or 'paralytic.'"[58] But the preservation of pluralities of truths does entail the very real possibility of being confronted with two competing hypotheses of equal strength and having to make a decision that appears as "forced, living, and momentous." Ryan not only alludes to the existentialism of Sartre in a way quite parallel to James's will to believe; he accuses Derrida of going too far, of being too anti-subjective.[59] Deconstruction is to be lauded for its criticism of the Cartesian/Husserlian subject; but there is nonetheless more of a self, through processive/progressive evolution, than one has in a Derridian analysis. Fragile and derivative as it may be, the processive self of James, making its decisions in fear and trembling, and in a spirit of seriousness, seems more cumulative than it is in Derrida,[60] though, to be fair, the style of James's activity changes from "existential" to "textual," that is, to writing as protest against inevitability.

A similar point about "seriousness" and the "will to believe" can be made by looking at the recent evaluation of John Dewey by the American philosopher Richard Rorty. To begin with, Rorty is clearly engaged in giving up the quest for certainty. In doing so, he purports to be arguing as a pragmatist, or at least as someone comfortable within the pragmatist tradition. "The great fallacy of the tradition, the pragmatists tell us, is to think that the metaphors of vision, correspondence, mapping, picturing, and representation which apply to small, routine assertions will apply to large and debatable ones."[61] In *Philosophy and the Mirror of Nature*, Rorty offers a more general synopsis of his position:

> Wittgenstein, Heidegger, and Dewey are in agreement that the notion of knowledge as accurate representation, made possible by special mental processes, and intelligible through a general theory of representation, needs to be abandoned. For all three, the notions of "foundations of knowledge" and of philosophy as revolving around the Cartesian attempt to answer the epistemological sceptic are set aside. . . . They set aside epistemology and metaphysics as possible disciplines.[62]

Such an approach does require Rorty to perform radical surgery on Dewey and James, since both of these thinkers did offer both an epistemology and a metaphysics. This he does not shrink from doing: "The Dewey of *Experience and Nature*, the James of *Radical Empiricism* . . . seem to me merely weakened versions of idealism."[63] And again, "Throughout his life, he [Dewey] wavered between a therapeutic stance toward philosophy and another, quite different, stance—one in which philosophy was to become 'scientific' and 'empirical' and to do something serious, systematic, important, and constructive." [64] When properly cauterized, Dewey's philosophy would be seen as, overall, playful or conversational, as opposed to serious. "Dewey's work helps us put aside that spirit of *seriousness* which artists traditionally lack and philosophers are traditionally supposed to maintain. For the spirit of seriousness can only exist in an intellectual world in which human life is an attempt to attain an end beyond life, an escape from freedom into the atemporal." [65]

Going further, Rorty, like Ryan, does not see the rejection of foundationalism or certainty as entailing the position of relativism. " 'Relativism' is the view that every belief on a certain topic, or perhaps about *any* topic, is as good as every other. No one holds this view. Except for the occasional cooperative freshman, one cannot find anybody who says that two incompatible opinions on an important topic are equally good. Those philosophers who get *called* 'relativists' are those who say that the grounds for choosing between such options are less algorithmic than had been thought." [66] Having disposed of relativism as a false issue, Rorty goes on to describe what he thinks is the major area of contention: "The real issue is not between people who think one view as good as another and people who do not. It is between those who think our culture or purpose, or intuitions cannot be supported except conversationally, and people who still hope for other sorts of support." [67] Again, there is much here that supports the antifoundationalism thesis of Dewey. But in addition, Rorty seems to have gone *from* the thesis that we do not have algorithmic grounds for anything *to* the conclusion that all we have is conversation. From a broader, more "traditional" Deweyian perspective, community now seems synonymous with conversation, and the only parameters of conversation are shaped by discourse. As with Derrida, here also "there is nothing outside the text." Context is important, but the text is the context. There are no existential constraints, only conversational constraints. "Socratic conversation is an activity which is its *own* end." [68] Success equals continuance or keeping up the conversation. Now there is a sense in which Rorty is right in his portrayal of James and Dewey here, namely, the sense in which for all of us in life "the nectar is in the journey," "it's not the victory but the battle," and so forth. (And indeed, I return to this sense and give Rorty credit in the Conclusion, below.) But this last way of putting it (the battle) brings up a point that Rorty sometimes underplays. Dewey was a social reformist, not simply a conversationalist; he viewed experience both as "*precarious* and as stable."⁶⁹ Going further, Rorty himself points out that James was exercising his own will to believe in holding that life feels like a real fight. At the end of *Pragmatism*, James tells the reader:

> I find myself willing to take the universe to be really dangerous and adventurous, without therefore backing out and crying "no play." . . . It is then perfectly possible to accept sincerely a drastic kind of a universe from which the element of "seriousness" is not to be expelled. Whoso does so is, it seems to me, a genuine pragmatist. He is willing to live on a scheme of uncertified possibilities which he trusts; willing to pay with his own person, if need be, for the realization of the ideals which he frames.⁷⁰

Rorty admits that life does feel like a real fight, but he puts this down to our being "footnotes" to Plato. "But," he asserts, "if James's own pragmatism were taken seriously, if pragmatism became central to our culture and our self-image, then it would no longer feel that way. We do not know how it *would* feel."⁷¹ But it is difficult to reconcile this thesis with the existentialist sense of the tragic found throughout James's works. Life is a game for James; it is the playing that counts. But in the Jamesian game not everyone wins; indeed, what makes hope possible also demands that the tragic be taken seriously. James asks the reader: "Does n't the fact of 'no' stand at the very core of life? Does n't the very 'seriousness' that we attribute to life mean that ineluctable noes and losses form a part of it, that there are genuine sacrifices somewhere, and that something permanently drastic and bitter always remains at the bottom of its cup?"[72] Rorty seems at times to realize that the same is true for Dewey. He chooses Dewey over Foucault, for example, because although they "are trying to do the same thing, Dewey seems . . . to have done it better, simply because his vocabulary allows room for unjustifiable hope, and an ungroundable but vital sense of human solidarity."[73] And again, "What Dewey suggested was that we keep the will to truth and the optimism that goes with it, but free them from the behaviorist notion that Behaviorese is Nature's Own Language *and* from the notion of man as 'transcendental or enduring subject.' For, in Dewey's hands, the will to truth is not the urge to dominate but the urge to create, to 'attain working harmony among diverse desires.' "[74]

Dewey did indeed strive to preserve a will to truth and tried consistently to avoid forms of domination associated with, for example, progress identified exclusively with a particular class struggle. His scientific/pragmatic method was a sustained attempt to attain gradualistic consensus. But the method is, at times, a bit too sanguine. Dewey's optimism about his method cannot deal with those Jamesian moments that are forced, living, and momentous. There is hope in Dewey, and the hope is unjustifiable from any foundationalist perspective; but hope exists only if reality is, in James's terms, "opaque," that is, only if the situation is not defined in advance as completely hopeless. As Graham Bird has noted, "James clearly associates a belief in free-will with the *hope* of making . . . a difference, but he recognises that that hope is quite fragile."[75] This point can be stated somewhat differently by turning to the issue of metaphysics. In the introduction to *Consequences of Pragmatism*, Rorty argues that the term "realism" "has come to be synonymous with 'anti-pragmatism.' "[76] Collapsing any forms of "technical realism" into variants of "intuitive realism," he argues that, for the latter, either "language does *not* go all the way down or, . . . contrary to the appearances, all vocabularies are commensurable."[77] Phrased in these terms, it would seem that, for James, language does *not* go all the way down, at least in some sense, and to credit it with accomplishing this task would be to succumb to "vicious intellectualism." Charlene Haddock Seigfried responds to Rorty's query about language in the following manner:

> In answer to what Rorty calls "a bedrock metaphilosophical issue;" namely, whether one can "ever appeal to nonlinguistic knowledge in philosophical argument," the answer is an unambiguous 'yes' and 'no.' 'No,' if this means outside of our meaning-giving organization of experience. 'Yes,' if this means outside of talking about talking. In addition to linguistic acts, we also act. We change situations, for better or worse, and not just our thinking/talking about them.[78]

In our terms, metaphysically for James, reality is not only broader than the (presently) known; it is broader than the know*able*. That is, our epistemic formulations will always leave something out, forcing us, at least sometimes, to act, with attendant "serious" consequences. Moreover, for Dewey, and also for Marx, reality is also broader than the known. Both were at times, however, tempted to accept the hypothesis that reality would, ultimately, be coextensive with the know*able*, that is, with what would be available if the proper method (pragmatism/partisanship) were carried out. Both, however, never seem to have completely felt comfortable with this position, and a reconstruction of their respective outlooks reveals that each requires a Jamesian "will to believe." In spite of recent assertions to the contrary, the context is broader than the text. As Thomas Nagel has noted in responding to Rorty's position, "unsolvable questions are not for that reason unreal."[79] Or as James put it so succinctly, "namelessness is compatible with existence."[80] But once again, while there is more than the text, the text itself is important. James is "naming the unnameable," so to speak. His use of language is a way of nurturing his own fragile self, and his textual product as invitation/provocation points beyond itself. The text does not go all the way down, but it becomes more and more important to James, as author. Finally, the text is at least quasi-serious; it is an attempt to be original, in an Emersonian sense.

PART THREE

APPLICATIONS

The classical American philosophers [e.g., William James] are . . . correctly understood as philosophers of experience, that is, as diagnosers of the flow of experience. They keep their eye on the irreducibly problematic character of our life in the world, and they attempt to float ideas which are assuaging and temporarily resolving. These philosophers are very chary of sheerly conceptual resolutions, demanding rather that their ideas "work," that is, are able to connect with the way in which experience is undergone and yet effect salutary change in the complex relationships between self and self, self and society, and self and nature. I call this the pragmatic upshot, by which I mean the detailing of the significance of imagination and speculation on the way in which we undergo our experiences.

JOHN J. MCDERMOTT, *Streams of Experience*

James is not a traditional philosopher by either temperament or training. Rather he is a cultural critic trained in medicine, fascinated with the arts, imbued with a scientific conscience, and attracted to religion. . . . He is neither afraid to traverse disciplinary boundaries nor hesitant to pronounce premature panaceas for centuries-old problems. In short, he is an authentic American intellectual frontiersman.

CORNEL WEST, *The American Evasion of Philosophy*

Chapter Seven

James and Modern Art: Process over Permanence

Although William James wrote no separate treatise on aesthetics, it does not follow from this that he had no opinion on art. Throughout his writings one finds continual one-line references to art, each of which is illuminating in itself. James himself turned to art first in his life. He was a good enough painter to consider this as a possible vocation. More important, the fact that he wrote no separate treatise on art might well indicate that he refused to separate art and life, or in other words, that the distinction between art and life was "vague" or "ambiguous." As his biographer Gay Wilson Allen has said, "William respected artistic creation as activity but not as artifact."[1]

In a letter to Theodore Flournoy, James made what is perhaps the most insightful of his concise statements on art. He asserted that a good thing about a work of art was its ability to tell "all sorts of things to different spectators, of none of which things the artist ever knew a word."[2] It would seem here that, for James, art was an ongoing process, open-ended enough to do justice to the "richness" of experience and, as unfinished, demanding the "intensity" of involvement and participation.[3]

In many ways James's philosophical views offer an insight into modern art. To show this, let us turn to the history of painting over the past century. No claim is made for completeness here; indeed, only a brief survey is possible.

In the following I shall begin, as modern art does, with the discrediting of the object. But I shall argue that the two conse- quent interpretations—art dealing with a higher object and art as emotional—are wrong. This can be seen by an analysis of con- temporary art itself. The initial result of discrediting the object was an inability to distinguish clearly any longer between art and — life. This is seen in art in the vast increase of media and techniques employed in aesthetic creation. Literally anything can have aes- thetic significance. The result of this interpenetration of art and life to the extent that all entities are (at least potentially) aesthetic has been a view of art as an *event,* a process still in the making. This too can be seen in modern art, especially in happenings, as- semblage, and the construction of environments. In brief, works of modern art are not objective, but they are more than subjec-— tive. They are ongoing events that endure through time. As such, from a Jamesian perspective, they both reflect and intensify, in the Greek sense of the term "mimesis," the ontological status of — "the vague."

Modern Art and the Discrediting of the Object

The discrediting of the object as something to be copied or imi- tated was a great step forward in the history of art. Although many factors contributed to its overthrow, the realization by the cubists that linear perspective placed a limitation of the possibilities for art was a major influence. The Renaissance approach to art advo- cated a complete, finished picture from a single point of view. The cubists included many points of view in their vision, and did so simultaneously. The cubists, then, refused to look at objects as a given whole; instead they analyzed objects into their basic geo- metrical patterns. These were broken into planes, which were collected in an interpenetrant pictorial concatenation. For example, in Pablo Picasso's *Les Demoiselles d'Avignon*, we are given a frontal image of two of the women, but a profile image of their noses. "Picasso and Braque, as the coinventors of cubism, . . . undertook a new definition of pictorial space in which objects were represented simultaneously from many visual angles, in wholes or in parts, opaque and transparent."[4]

The first effect of this procedure is to discredit the object, since many visions of the so-called object are given at once, and no one of them predominates. "In Cubist art, for the first time in Western painting, . . . [the] guiding model disappears."[5] The painting is no longer conditioned by an impartial object to which it "refers." Juan Gris wrote: " 'Until the work is completed, the painter must remain ignorant of its appearance as a whole.' "[6] There is no one object to refer to. Rather are there a series of ways of taking or appropriating an object. Beyond these appropriations, we cannot actually ask what there is. The cubist, by refusing to adopt only one perspectival stance, is emphasizing that there is no one given objective way in which to see reality.

This school of art, though central, had certain predecessors. Impressionism, for example, though still object-centered, had become aware of the influence of light. Claude Monet's *Rouen Cathedral* (1892–94), for instance, is a series of superimpositions or variations of the "same" building, at about the same angle. Clearly, Monet's intention in the work is to illustrate the effect his subject would produce at different times of the day, in good or bad weather, in different seasons, and so forth. "Never before had anyone changed their position so little and discovered so many facets in a single subject; or rather, never before had anyone caught with such sensibility the miraculous and multiple reality of light and atmosphere."[7] While impressionism as such maintained a form of realism, the fact remains that the basic given in experience is not simply "the object" but rather the object-in-this-light, the object-in-that-light, and so forth, and most important, these cannot be reduced. There is no basic given below these, and these are concatenated. They share a certain "family resemblance" but they are not monistic. Once again, one can see the "myth of the given" beginning to be criticized.

The pointillist style of painting employed by neoimpressionism gained a momentum of its own. For some artists, color began to be taken as an object in itself, with the result that one group received the name *Les Fauves* (the wild beasts) because of their unrestrained use of color. From the realization that light entered every object, the fauves moved to a position that upheld the importance of color contrasts rather than duplicating the color of the object. The intense preoccupation with the spectrum of object-in-a-given-light achieved a heightened awareness of the possibilities of color. The fauves freed color from any "relation to the outside world, . . . [and] also . . . [from] relation to the rules to which their predecessors felt it was necessarily tied. To indicate shadows, they did not only use cold colours, but on occasions even purple or red. As for complementary colours, they did not use them systematically; they looked for unusual harmonies and were not deterred by stridency or dissonances."[8]

Henri Matisse, for example, was initially characterized as a fauve. In his *Blue Window*, we are given a still life that blends right into a landscape; it is difficult to distinguish the various perceptual planes within the picture. Everything is "squashed up" onto the canvas, and the important thing is the interplay of colors. When we expect to find spatial planes, we find instead several planes at once. Again, the object as a given is discredited, and we are given in its stead several possible viewings of the object. The art commentator W. Fleming notes that "in this picture, Matisse came close to realizing his dream of an 'art of balance, of purity and serenity devoid of depressing subject matter.'"[9]

Simultaneously with fauvism, German expressionism also criticized the object as a given. Wassily Kandinsky became the foremost figure of the southern German expressionist movement but was soon to move out of it to the realm of nonobjective art. Kandinsky eliminated objects and figures from his art by 1913, and in this sense he pointed the way toward the abstract expressionism of Jackson Pollock in the 1940s. Art is "liberated" from the object entirely, and this opens up a whole series of possibilities—as well as, admittedly, some dangers. The question must be asked, What will replace the object? Many thought colors and shapes would and concluded from this either that art would be the formal interplay of colors *or* that art would simply be the expression of emotion via brilliant colors. Both of these, however, are reactions based on old schemas. Kandinsky himself gives us a hint about the better criteria to be used once the object is cast aside. "Commenting on his completely abstract paintings, Kandinsky stated that their content is 'what the spectator *lives* or *feels* while under the effect of the *form and color combinations* of the picture.' " [10] Here we note the implicit assertion that art is really an activity or a process, not a replacing of one object by another one or a replacing of "objectivity" by "subjectivity." With Kandinsky, "an element of uncertainty entered modern art. Are our interpretations right? Are our value judgments correct? These are the disturbing questions we ask as we face a work of art incommensurable with nature and disconnected from tradition." [11]

All of these instances have one thing in common. They have all agreed that the object as a given is no longer an adequate reference point for the artist. To be sure, they have drawn different conclusions from this thesis. Impressionism maintains that it is copying a new fluid world, and in this sense it asserts that it is a realism. Expressionism, with its emphasis on colors and lights, upholds the world of emotion and the displaying of psychological states. Abstractionism, concluding that the subject as encountered is illusory, reduces it to its geometrical elements and takes these cold, immutable, and eternal entities as the new reality. From the fact that the object has been discredited, however, it does not necessarily follow *either* that painting must be subjective *or* that a new object must replace the old one. This point can be developed in two ways. First of all, by highlighting the connection between art and life: the latter is neither an object nor, since it is partly continuous, simply subjective. This leads naturally into my second point, namely, the assertion that art is an activity or a process and as such cannot be judged by the labels "subjective" and "objective."

The discrediting of the object has the immediate effect of multiplying the possible objects that can be called "art." If there is no one given standard to imitate, anything could, conceivably, become aesthetic. The futurists, for example, a group developing simultaneously with cubism and sharing many of its techniques, wanted to destroy the whole idea of museum art. Futurists were fascinated by the contemporary age of machinery, motion, speed, and velocity. In *Manifesto of Futurist Painters* in 1909, Filippo Marinetti listed their aim as that of praising " 'aggressive movement, feverish insomnia, a quick pace, the perilous leap.' " [12] " 'A roaring motor-car, which runs like a machine gun,' they said, 'is more beautiful than the Winged Victor of Samothrace.' " [13] Again and again, in the futurist drawings we see two things emphasized: the pervasiveness of aesthetic experience and the concern with motion, speed, or, in short, time.

Futurist art highlighted the age of machinery and its aesthetic dimension. Life was "mechanical" in the sense that the personal had no "safe" place in it. Art is not objective, since it emphasizes the importance of motion rather than permanence. " 'Who can still believe in the opacity of bodies?' Marinetti wrote in 1910." [14] In addition, however, art is not subjective, since the very notion of a subject has also been discredited. Apparently, then, the futurists, through emphasizing the pervasiveness of aesthetic experience, have, perhaps inadvertently, pointed out the inadequacy of "objective" and "subjective" as characterizations of their art.

The most blatant statement that art could no longer be distinguished from life came from dada. Although partly the product of the horror induced by World War I, dada did leave an important message for art. This message is most adequately seen in the work of Marcel Duchamp, who asserted that *any* object could attain the level of art. His "ready-mades" have become famous. For example, he purchased a urinal, which he signed "R. Mutt," entitled it *The Fountain*, and sent it to the Society of Independent Artists in New York in 1917.

Duchamp's point here is obvious; even the trivial can become aesthetic. Art no longer can claim a superiority to life, because there is no complete distinction between art and life. The importance of chance, or uncertainty, was always found in his works. The traditional approach to art he considered a habit-forming drug, which as such had no veracity, or truth.[15] He was opposed to absolute standards of weights and measures in art. In one creation, *Standard Stops*, he dropped a thread from a height of one meter, fixed the shape it assumed in varnish, and used this shape as his standard for the piece. Calvin Tomkins catches this point well. "The whole idea of chance, which was later to become the indispensable tool of a number of artists who saw it as a means to make their work conform more closely to the conditions of life, interested Duchamp in a rather unique way."[16] Since everything is uncertain, anything could be lifted to the level of art. Or, more positively stated, life itself is, at least potentially, aesthetic. This position, once again, is neither objective nor subjective. The creative act for Duchamp was not completed by the artist. As he himself said, "All in all, the creative act is not performed by the artist alone; the spectator brings the work in contact with the external world by deciphering and interpreting its inner qualifications and thus adds his contribution to the creative act. This becomes even more obvious when posterity gives its final verdict and sometimes rehabilitates forgotten artists."[17]

The work of art, then, is unfinished, and only insofar as it is "taken" or appropriated by the spectator/participator does an aesthetic experience endure. This appropriation process is continuous. The artist, in initiating an act of creation, is not aware of its final outcome. As such the work of art is uncertain, because there is no final object it has to copy, no final form or essence it has to approach. The artist no longer has personal control over his or her material. The extension of the number of things ("ready-mades") that could become art to the stage where life could be called "artistic" has had profound results for aesthetics. L. Meyer, in his original introduction to *The Bride and the Bachelors*, sees the approach of such people as Duchamp as involving a new aesthetics of "radical empiricism," its basis being

a new conception of man and the universe, which is almost the opposite of the view that has dominated Western thought since its beginnings. . . . Man is no longer the center of the universe. . . . Radical empiricist art reflects the loss of belief in man's ability to control nature or his own destiny; it finds support in the contemporary scientific revolution, which has shown . . . that nature's processes are inherently indeterminate, unpredictable, and ultimately unknowable. . . . And radical empiricist art therefore refuses to be goal oriented, or teleological.[18]

For dada, in brief, life was artistic, in the sense that anything could be art. But life was also uncertain, challenging, not something one had full control over, but rather something a person found himself or herself involved with, and as unfinished, was forced to create, shape, and mold. We are all artists, if Duchamp is right, because we all live in an uncertain world where we are forced to be creative.

Neodadaism, the pop art of the 1960s, is a continuation of this trend, without the despair of World War I. As Robert Rauschenberg has said, art is not an end in itself, but simply a " 'means to function thoroughly and passionately in a world that has a lot more to it than paint.' "[19] Pop art in general has celebrated living—not one section of life as was the traditional way of painting, but rather the day-to-day living involving television, commercials, comic strips, hot dogs, and so on. The pop movement took its aesthetic from the commonplace and sought the beauty concealed in the vulgar and the banal. With its roots in the ready-mades of Duchamp, pop art celebrated with a universal intensity the art of living. Pop artists share "an intense passion for direct experience, for unqualified participation in the richness of our immediate world, whatever it may have become, for better or worse."[20] An artist like Rauschenberg will create a collage of juxtaposed diverse elements, such as a pillow, a shirt, a stuffed eagle, a skirt, and so forth. In this way he tries to create a picture that obliterates the line between art and life.[21] In Rauchenberg's view, the work of art is not separated from the real world by a frame. *Tracer*, for example, is a "combine" of various trash objects, such as automobile tires, umbrellas, bicycle wheels, and so on. The entrance into the work of "found" objects from outside "breaks down the distinction between a shirt collar, say, as an article of clothing and the same thing as an emotive pictorial device. In other words, we begin to operate here in an indeterminate area somewhere between art and life."[22]

This same message, the celebration of life as aesthetic through the use of more and more diverse media, can be found in the work of Claus Oldenburg. Something as common as a hamburger becomes "a complex, multileveled symbol" in his work. It can stand as an expression of our time, reflect cars, travel, highways, or roadside stands. It is "simple" enough to be truly multidimensional. Most important, it is not simply a copy of a given object. John Rublowsky relates the story of a visitor to Oldenburg's studio who picked up an object that Oldenburg had made, a vaguely shaped piece of plaster in the form of a wedge.[23] The visitor had great difficulty in calling it a lady's handbag first, then an iron, then a typewriter, then a toaster, finally a piece of pie. "Oldenburg was delighted. The object, which was nothing more than a shape the artist had been toying with, was exactly what the visitor had described. All the objects he named were embodied in that small, wedge-shaped bit of painted plaster."[24] This uncertainty resulting from the discrediting of the object is what enables Oldenburg, Duchamp, and others to highlight the connection between art and life. It is precisely because there is no object that all entities can be seen as, at least potentially, aesthetic. As Oldenburg himself put it, " 'I am for an art that takes its form from the lines of life, that twists and extends impossibly and accumulates and spits and drips and is as sweet and stupid as life itself.' "[25] Nothing, in short, is exempt from becoming an object of art, because nothing is objective, that is, finished. Pop art raises the question as to whether or not we are willing to let life become art.

Sandwiched in between the two instances of dadaism was surrealism, or literally superrealism, which asserted that a greater reality could be found beneath the apparent objective world. There was, in brief, more to life than the logical physical world we are conscious of. Apprehended objects are actually fringed by an illogical subconscious periphery. In many of the works of Salvador Dali, for example, we are confronted with double and triple images. Depending on how close or far away from the painting we stand, we are given one view, then a second, and so forth. Surrealism too took the discrediting of the object at face value, with the result that no clear distinction could be made between art and life. The images in Dali's works actually change their meaning before our very eyes.

As a result, our own point of view begins to vacillate. As André Breton writes: "A tomato is also a child's balloon—Surrealism, I repeat, having suppressed the word *like*."[26] "Like" is suppressed because there is no fixed reference point. Uncertainty is reflected in the lack of any clear-cut distinction between illusion and reality.

In all of these views, one sees the discrediting of the object pushed one step further—to the inability to distinguish between what is art and what is "natural." Uncertainty is a theme common to all of these positions. Futurism highlights the interpenetration of art and life by its fascination with machinery and its depersonification of experience: in addition, dada emphasized the inability of a culture to emphasize "museum art" any longer. Duchamp's ready-mades indicate clearly that anything can be called art and that art is uncertain, the act of creation being still unfinished. Pop art continues this theme, celebrating the richness of life itself, by breaking down the distinction between art and experience. Surrealism, with its assertion that physical objects are subconsciously fringed by past experience, highlights the same fact.

The first reaction to this refusal to accept a given object and the consequent inability to distinguish artificial and natural art and life might be to term *all* art subjective; since no common reference point can be agreed on, it would seem possible that all opinions concerning art are necessarily relegated to the status of private whim. Indeed, some of the schools we have looked at above have interpreted their art in this way. The fauves, for example, considered their work to be emotive. Dada was taken to be a sheer emotional nihilism—destruction for the sake of destruction. Pop art for many was simply a put-on—interesting, but possessing no cognitive value.

It is not necessary to move from the fact that objectivity is a myth to the conclusion that all outlooks are equally subjective, however. Indeed, such categories betray a commitment to traditional "substantialist" metaphysics and make no sense in the Jamesian ever-changing world of concatenated "pure experience." In short, such either/or terminology as that of the subject/object dichotomy fails to take account of the fundamental property of time and endurance *through* (not above) time in a work of art. Let us turn, then, to the description of art as a process or a temporal event.

Modern Art as Process

As far back as impressionism, we can see the importance of temporal process. Monet's cathedral can be seen in several different ways because of the temporal play of light on the structure. Strictly speaking, then, the work is still in the making. There is an ongoing series of ways to view the cathedral, and these run into one another.

Matisse's *Blue Window* has the same emphasis; the hatpins in the picture "run into" the empty vase; the flowers in the vase "grow into" the foliage outside the window, and so on. Again, the interpenetration of points of view highlights the work as a process.

Cubism, with its simultaneous portrayal of many different geometrical points of view superimposed on a canvas, created the notion of the work of art as an activity. The importance of motion in the futurist and cubist paintings emphasizes over and over again the actual temporality of the aesthetic experience. The cubist theory of vision emphasized the temporal complexity of life; in trying to view a cubist work, we are forced to become participators in a temporal process.

This same point was made by Duchamp in advocating dada. The work of art is unfinished by the artist; it is continually re-created by the spectators. Surrealism, with its emphasis on the interpenetrating fringes of experience, also highlights the temporal effect. Indeed, one might say that the discrediting of the object took place simultaneously with the assertion that art was a process, not an object. As such it is the activity of artistic creation that aesthetics is concerned with, not any given collection of paint dabs on a canvas. Gillo Dorfles has caught this point extremely well. "Today—or from the beginning of the technological era— *speed* is basic to our life or relationships. Pressured by continuous dynamic impulses, surrounded by an incessant tide of motion, we have become dominated by this new dimension; often we can succeed in conceiving of life and its 'products' only as evolving in a continuous and persistent *becoming*."[27]

This emphasis on experience as a process, on becoming as more important than being, was paramount in James's outlook. We have seen him refer again and again to the unfinished character of the universe. In contemporary art also we find becoming emphasized. The action painting of Jackson Pollock, as seen in paintings involving the famous dripping technique, continues to emphasize the notion of art as an event. This artist actually placed his canvas on the floor in order to move into his pictures as a participator. In paintings such as *Convergence*, for example, there is no predetermined goal; rather, it is the actual act of painting that becomes the content of aesthetic experience. As Neumeyer notes, in coming upon a work of Pollock's, "we ourselves, endowed with an organizing vision, tend to infuse meaning into a painting, instinctively seeing form and expression wherever there is movement upon a surface. Thus it is hard to say where Pollock's work ends and ours begins."[28] Again, we are given the same message as in Duchamp's work—art is an activity, a quasi-continuous one, not an atomistic bundle of unrelated pieces. The human contribution cannot be weeded out, either on the side of the artist or on the side of the participator.

"Op art," another form of action painting, carries this same message. Optical art forces action to take place in the viewer's eyes. Using such techniques as checkerboard environs and afterimages, optical art has forced the spectator to become a temporal participator in the activity of art.

Finally, in the actual creation of "environments" and "happenings" we have the most blatant indication of the interpenetration of art and the "external" world, and the consequent realization that art is a process. In his "Manifesto on Happenings," Alan Kaprow rejects the traditional history of art and of aesthetics, and notes that the old questions of absolute definitions and standards of excellence are irrelevant. "The contemporary artist is not out to supplant recent modern art with a better kind; *he wonders what art might be*. Art and life are not simply commingled; *their identities are both uncertain*."[29]

Happenings, as such, are unfinished; they are continuous and involve everyone who comes on them. We not only see a happening, we walk through it, participate in it, are confronted by it. A happening takes time; it is, to be sure, uncertain, since it has no fixed goal, but it is also a slowly developing process. Karrow states elsewhere: "Assemblages and Environments . . . [have] at root the same . . . principle . . . *extension*. Molecule-like, the materials . . .

at one's disposal grow in any desired direction and take on any shape whatsoever. In the finest of these works the field, therefore, is created as one goes along, rather than being there *a priori*, as in the case of a canvas of certain dimensions. It is a process."[30]

This point—the importance of "becoming" in art—is re-affirmed by the use of perishable materials to construct a work. Several works are self-destructive; others are constructed of newspaper, adhesive tape, and so forth. In one form of environmental construction, "earth art," the earth itself is used as a medium. For example, several "artists" assembled and "aesthetically claimed" the coastal cliffs of Australia by wrapping them in cloth.[31] In works such as these, it is the idea of doing, of acting, that counts; there is no finished product. As Kaprow says:

> There is no fundamental reason why . . . [the art work] should be a fixed, enduring object to be placed in a locked case. The spirit does not require the proofs of the embalmer. If one cannot pass this work on to his children in the form of a piece of "property," the attitudes and values it embodies surely can be transmitted. And like so many quite acceptable but passing facets of our lives, this art can be considered as a semi-intangible entity, something to be renewed in different forms like fine cooking or the seasonal changes, which we do not put into our pockets, but need nevertheless.[32]

In brief, the object has been discredited, but art is not simply subjective. Rather must art be taken as an ongoing process, uncertain, and therefore intense, but at least somewhat continuous, and therefore more than simply subjective. Modern art gives us a picture of a processive environment in which "the subject-object duality is no longer to the point, for at both ends these terms are but abstract statements of actually dynamic processes."[33]

Both characteristics (subjective and objective) are inadequate to describe the *activity* of modern art. Unfortunately, much of this has been missed by critics remaining within the old categories, that is, either that art is objective or that it is subjective. If objective, it supposedly aims at a reality "higher" than the physical, namely, that of shape and form. If not objective, then subjective, that is, merely the emotional evocation or expression of the artist. All of the above-mentioned art movements may have particular difficulties of their own, but they agree on one thing: the physical object can no longer be taken as a given. Also, in place of this they seem to be putting art as process, activity, or event. Time has become a crucial category in art.

Conclusion

In earlier chapters I explicated William James's philosophy in terms of vagueness, richness, and intensity. Both James and modern art have the same beginning: the discrediting of the object. There are no absolutes in James, and there are no "givens" in art. They also share the same reaction to this rejection. Life for James is not simply subjective, if subjective means doing whatever one wants whenever one wants. Experience is a process, as yet unfinished, but nonetheless continuous. For art too the rejection of objectivity leads not to subjectivity but to the recognition of art as an event or process. From impressionism to environments and happenings, this point has been developed. It would seem useful, then, to apply the notions of vagueness, richness, and intensity to modern art also.

An aesthetic of modern art, when so judged, would have to deal with the enduring quality of a work of art. Since there is no given object, nor indeed any one way to take or apprehend an object, those works of art would be most highly prized that were open-ended enough to reflect the multidimensionality of experience. Not only can anything potentially be termed a work of art, but each "thing" has many dimensions. In dealing with life, now seen as a process, a contemporary aesthetic would have to be open to the richness of experience. Further, the very "tentativeness" of objects would force us to choose, to make a difference, to be committed. A work of art, in order to be significant, should not only be vague enough to be interpreted in several different ways, each one "meaningful" in its own right, but should also make observers aware of the fact that they are being forced to interpret or re-create the "object" being presented. (In an important sense, I have argued that James's own texts need to be "taken" in this way, as "vague," and I return to this in the conclusion.)

In this way a modern aesthetic would be one of process, and as such would deal with a continuing, ongoing interaction among artist, appropriated object, and observers, who in actuality are co-artists.[34] On the one hand, all objects are potentially works of art, since they can be aesthetically "claimed." Even the earth, as we saw above, can function as a medium. On the other hand, the use of vagueness, richness, and intensity as evaluative categories also enables us to establish a relative hierarchy of aesthetic objects. A work of art, as a process, would have to challenge the co-artists, confront them, perhaps even shock them. But shock for the sake of shock would be a rather impoverished experience. The intensity of a work must be taken together with its cumulative dimension, its richness, its ability to reflect the jewellike quality of experience, which can sparkle in many different ways. Those creations rich enough to be interpreted in several ways, each significant, and yet relevant enough to force a decision, or a series of partially overlapping decisions from different people, would be deemed most significant. The actual aesthetic experience would be the process of growth. Shakespeare's works, then, would be deemed great art because they are *vague,* that is, rich enough to be taken in many different ways, and yet pressing enough to make us aware of the intense experience of selecting which interpretation to opt for. In other words, "contemporary art does not tend to create objects of honor. Rather, it honors the act of creating."[35] A relative hierarchy of these "actings," however, is possible in terms of richness

and intensity. Those creative acts are most aesthetically significant which, in their presentation of experience, do justice to its
richness and involve the viewer/reader in the aesthetic process. To
be sure, there is no way of picking up an object and determining
beforehand exactly what its level on the aesthetic scale will be.
The proof of the pudding in modern art, as in James, is decidedly
in the eating. One can, however, create works of art that reflect
back on themselves. One can, in other words, create a work that
is consciously and concretely vague enough to be taken in different ways, even though these appropriations are both cumulative
and intense. It is this type of creation that seems to be going on in
many areas today.

In sum, modern art in general has become interested in activity as a process. "Speaking in broad terms, modern art has
attempted to upend the fixed character of aesthetic values and of
late has contended that any material and any technique, given a
relational context, can bring forth a work of art."[36] The discrediting of the object has resulted in the lack of distinction between
art and life or nature. Life in our century has been recognized as a
process, still in the making. Modern art reflects and intensifies this
realization. The real work of art is the ongoing process among artist, aesthetically claimed object, and viewer/reader. This is itself
the event, and as such it is unfinished. Those events are better
which allow for more rich experiences at a more intense level. As
Amy Golden said in *Art News*, "Artists nowadays are bypassing
art in favor of a sort of noiseless spiritual happening. The things
they make are less art or objects than experiences. The sociological
wheels roll on. Museums exhibit what they call style, collectors
buy what they call art—but the basic enterprise has been replaced.
Some of the freshest minds of our times have given up on art and
gone on to making vehicles for aesthetic experience."[37]

These aesthetic experiences, or better, events, can be judged
in terms of vagueness, richness, and intensity. They must challenge
and confront us, but they must do so in a continuous, relational
manner. Those works of art termed "great" have been able to en-

dure via re-creation *through* time, not above it. They have been able to do so because they have been continually re-created, continually appropriated at different levels by various viewers for various purposes. They have kept open to the richness of experience without losing their cutting edge.

Art has been declared an activity rather than an artifact in our century. As such it needs new categories, new methods of evaluation. Neither subjectivity nor objectivity is an adequate label to apply to modern art. If James's inclination to art never left him completely, and if my analysis of his overall outlook in terms of vagueness, richness, and intensity is warranted, it would seem apropos to try these categories as new ones capable of doing justice to the temporal character of modern art. To be sure, no estimations can be made for certain in advance. To assert that they could would be to go contrary to the entire Jamesian denial of objectivity. But these new categories, tentatively assumed, might at least "unstiffen" things a little, that is, they might thaw some overly "static" interpretations of modern art currently in use.

Chapter Eight

Vagueness and Empathy in Medicine: A Jamesian View

In the fifth lecture in *Pragmatism*, William James makes the following statement:

> There are . . . at least three well-characterized levels, stages, or types of thought about the world we live in, and the notions of one stage have one kind of merit, those of another stage another kind. It is impossible, however, to say that any stage as yet in sight is absolutely more *true* than any other. Common sense is the more *consolidated* stage, because it got its innings first, and made all language into its ally. Whether it or science [the second stage] be the more *august* stage may be left to private judgment. But neither consolidation nor augustness are decisive marks of truth. . . . Vainly did scholasticism, common sense's college-trained younger sister, seek to stereotype the forms the human family had always talked with, to make them definite and fix them for eternity. . . .
>
> There is no *ringing* conclusion possible when we compare these types of thinking, with a view to telling which is the more absolutely true. . . . Common sense is *better* for one sphere of life, science for another, philosophic criti-

cism for a third; but whether either be *truer* absolutely, Heaven only knows. . . . Profusion, not economy, may after all be reality's key-note.[1]

This chapter is an attempt to extend and defend this affirmation of profusion.[2] As we have seen, overflowing vagueness may well be the central thread in the Jamesian corpus, having an epistemic and an ontological dimension—as well as others. Furthermore, empathy arises as a problem precisely in those situations wherein vagueness has been lost or is viewed as unimportant. In each of these three areas—common sense, science, and philosophy—empathy can, and has, become an issue. But the relationships among these three areas are complex and must be carefully spelled out. Empathy arises as an issue *through* the conceptual-linguistic world views of science and philosophy. Originally, as Alfred Schutz has shown,[3] the world of the ordinary is inherently intersubjective. Once the alternate types of reality found in science and philosophy have been "formed," however, they are themselves "formative." That is, they can and have in turn "infected" the world of common sense. The net result of this development is that no level or type of reality is sufficient, though all are necessary. James at times recognized this. In Chapter Four, it was shown that reality is beyond any linguistic formulation, yet it is accessible only through such formulations. This metaphysical stance has an important effect on the issue of empathy. The meaning of empathy can be elucidated on each of the three levels mentioned above; however, these conceptual analyses reveal that empathy is a "never-to-be-completely-grounded" state. For James, something is always left out of conceptualization; "ever not quite" trails along after every attempt. What is left out is, quite simply, action. The idea or meaning of "empathy" is not the *act* of empathy, is not empathizing. Nevertheless, conceptual analyses of the empathetic are now unavoidable because we are embedded in language, in "pure" consciousness, so to speak. As a result, empathy appears epistemically as an issue unsolvable in terms of certainty, and empathy appears ontologically as an issue that compels action.

The enemy of the vague or mysterious, both ontologically and epistemically, is the certain, the objective, or the immediate. The following pages describe the loss of vagueness, and hence the problematic nature of empathy, as it appears on the commonsense level, the level of science (specifically, of medicine viewed as science), and the level of philosophy. Finally, using James's views on language, metaphysics, and the affective dimension, I argue for the preservation of the vague on each of these three levels.

The Everyday World in Trouble Because of Immediacy

If we look at several critics of American "culture," or the way we have and undergo our experience in the everyday world, a curious fact emerges. Behind the various verbalizations of the problematic, and the alternatives envisioned, critics are charging that Americans are in trouble because of the quest for immediacy. I select four critics at random, for purposes of illustration. No claim for completeness is made.

In his work *The Pursuit of Loneliness: American Culture at the Breaking Point*, the sociologist Philip Slater charges that contemporary American culture systematically represses three fundamental human needs. First, it stifles the human need for community, and advocates instead the continual pursuit of private homes, private rooms, private cars—in short, the insulated wrap-around space of the chrysalis. One result of this is that interpersonal contact, not being sought or intended, is often abrasive.

Next, Slater charges that contemporary culture denies the human need for engagement with a situation or problematic. We ignore problems as long as possible, refuse to estimate their long-term ramifications, and ultimately try to "solve" multidimensional issues monochromatically—that is, via technology. We solve urban renewal issues via technical blueprints and then react angrily when the seemingly well-worked-out solution fails.

Finally, American culture downgrades the need for interdependence, and from childhood on fosters internal emotional control mechanisms in each individual. While this may solve some problems, it ultimately results in individuals who are never able to give themselves "wholeheartedly" in a situation.

Even a cursory glance at these criticisms reveals that they are concerned with variations of the I-Thou experience. Slater's general charge, then, is that we are systematically repressing the I-Thou experience, which takes place only in a vague or mysterious context; we do so to the extent that, if we are confronted with these (repressed) needs, we tend to respond with physical violence. Slater verbalizes this loss of mystery in his charge that decisions in America are dominated by the "toilet principle":

> Our ideas about institutionalizing the aged, psychotic, retarded, and infirm are based on a pattern of thought that we might call the *Toilet Assumption*—the notion that unwanted matter, unwanted difficulties, unwanted complexities and obstacles will disappear if they are removed from our immediate field of vision. . . . The result of our social efforts has been to remove the underlying problems of our society farther and farther from daily experience and daily consciousness, and hence to decrease, in the mass of the population, the knowledge, skill, resources, and motivation necessary to deal with them.[4]

In *The Making of a Counter Culture*, Theodore Roszak charges that we are in trouble because we have become a "technocracy," that is, a society inextricably beholden to experts. Experts, if challenged, fall back on science; science falls back on objectivity. For Roszak, if one attempts to question objectivity, one is labeled by default "subjective," "quaint," "irrational," or just plain "mad." In short, one is relegated to the "cultural garbage can."

In such a society where the "myth of objective consciousness" is cultivated, an "in here/out there" dichotomy is adopted. In order to look qua spectator for objectivity, one must go through the whole "emptying out" process. Optimally, there is to be no personal investment of the self in the act of awareness; the ideal state of affairs is to have an empty egoic "in here" objectively analyzing the "out there." We also, Roszak charges, adopt an invidious hierarchy; the "in here," which is relied on and trusted, tries to control and manipulate the "out there." Finally, we try to do this as mechanically as possible. Ultimately, the egoic is reduced to a steady, repeatable electronic nervous system.

Roszak's claim consists in the thesis that the psychology of "scientific consciousness depreciates our capacity for wonder by progressively estranging us from the magic of the environment."[5] It is his belief that "mystery . . . as the non-human dimension of reality . . . served to enrich the lives of men by confronting them with a realm of inexhaustible wonder."[6] Arguing ostensively, he offers the shaman as a model for reinstating the magical world of the I-Thou, or intersubjective experience.

In an influential work entitled *Habits of the Heart*, Robert Bellah, Richard Madsen, William M. Sullivan, Ann Swidler, and Steven M. Tipton ask "whether individualism, as the dominant ideology of American life, is not undermining the conditions of its existence."[7] Lamenting the language of abstract, that is, exclusionary, "ontological individualism" as limiting the ways in which people think, they note that it "would be well for us to rejoin the human race,"[8] and suggest that at the heart of our problem is a basic bifurcation of experience not unlike the one decried by Roszak.

> The most important boundary that must be transcended
> is the recent and quite arbitrary boundary between the
> social sciences and the humanities. The humanities, we are

told, have to do with the transmission and interpretation of cultural traditions in the realms of philosophy, religion, literature, language, and the arts, whereas the social sciences involve the scientific study of human action. The assumption is that the social sciences are not cultural traditions but rather occupy a privileged position of pure observation. The assumption is also that discussions of human action in the humanities are "impressionistic" and "anecdotal" and do not really become knowledge until "tested" by the methods of science, from which alone comes valid knowledge.[9]

In opposition, these authors do not see social science as value-free, but rather as a public philosophy of self-interpretation. Moreover, the interpretation they offer, as participatory members of the context they are studying, prioritizes the need to recover the insights of the older biblical and republican traditions.

What is at issue is not simply whether self-contained individuals might withdraw from the public sphere to pursue purely private ends, but whether such individuals are capable of sustaining either a public *or* a private life. If this is the danger, perhaps only the civic and biblical forms of individualism—forms that see the individual in relation to a larger whole, a community and a tradition—are capable of sustaining genuine individuality and nurturing both public and private life.[10]

Most significantly, the authors specifically connect the religious dimension with a need to regain a sense of wonder. As they put it, "perhaps common worship, in which we express our gratitude and wonder in the face of the mystery of being itself, is the most important thing of all."[11]

Finally, consider the work of Joseph Campbell, who for decades tirelessly pointed out the importance of myth for human existence. "If a *differentiating* feature is to be named, separating human from animal psychology, it is surely this of the subordination in the human sphere of even economics to mythology." [12] For Campbell, "myth is metaphor",[13] and should not be confused with ideology. Like Bellah and his coauthors, Campbell is concerned with including the heart in any analysis. "Myths don't count if they're just hitting your rational faculties—they have to hit the heart." [14] While mythology can be viewed as an expression of the collective unconscious, it does not provide answers in terms of rational certainty, but rather discloses some commonalities in human experience beyond the immediately apparent. More specifically, mythologies, when properly functioning, have the following aspects. First, they preserve in us a sense of awe about the mystery of the universe and our relationship to it; second, myths stem from the recognition of our own mortality. They guide us through the stages of life, from childhood to old age, and finally, to the deathbed. But myths also tend to support the endurance of the social order through rites and rituals, and hence, in some sense, they allow for the transcendence of individual mortality; finally, myths provide an understanding of the universe in general accord with the science of the time.[15]

But for Campbell, the old myths are no longer operative, and we are now under the burden of trying to create and discover their new incarnations. Such a procedure will not lead to one grand mythology, but rather to pluralism. Furthermore, Campbell's assertion that we need myth seen as metaphor precludes any foregrounding of the immediate. As metaphor, the "myth does not point to a fact; the myth points beyond facts to something that informs the fact." [16]

To be sure, there are no complete answers in these four scenarios. Indeed, they are sometimes more descriptive than they are explanatory. They do indicate, however, that several critics of our culture fault us for having lost, or at least being in danger of losing, a sense of vagueness or mystery and replacing it with a world of immediacy.

Similar criticisms are made by Daniel Boorstin, who believes that America is sick because it has no past, having replaced the study of history with social studies,[17] and by Harvey Cox, who asserts that "festivity" and "fantasy," that is, appropriation of the past in celebration, and dreams about the future, are essential aspects of human nature. Both, of course, require transcending the immediacy of the present moment.[18] The common theme of these criticisms is, once again, fear of a bewitchment with immediacy; with no sense of the past or of the future, we are locked in the eternal present. In short, the everyday world is now under the spell of the immediate, although not completely conscious of this fact. What appears as common sense is, in actuality, a predetermined theory that holds that the certain, the immediate, the objective is real, and the vague, the profuse, the ambiguous, false. It is on the level of philosophy and science that this penchant for immediacy became a *conscious* endeavor, and it is from these two levels that immediacy has filtered down into the world of common sense.

Immediacy in Philosophy

That immediacy has been predominant in several modern philosophical outlooks is not news. The history of the quest-for-certainty debate between the rationalists and the empiricists bears this out. René Descartes explicitly identified knowledge with certainty in his *Meditations*, and identified the latter with self-evident truths, innate ideas, immediately available and self-justifying to the rational light of the intellect. The rationale and defense of a priori propositions, predicated on the "inconceivability of the opposite," is a continuation of this point of view. The empiricist tradition accepted Descartes' question, What do I know for sure? but answered it differently. Sure knowledge comes through sensation. The latter is simple and immediate or noninferential. It is when inferences are made via associating various sensations or guessing at their cause that mistakes can be made. In short, common to both traditions are the propositions that something is *immediately* given and that what is so given constitutes, apodictic, certain knowledge. The possibility that what is present at the primordial level is *not* immediate, that is, that there is no noninferential level, is not condoned.

It is not without reason, then, that the I-Thou or intersubjective experience is so hard to locate or deal with in these two traditions. To view the intersubjective as basic would be to assert that the basic is not simple. God is dealt with more as a proposition than a person in Descartes. George Berkeley has considerable difficulty recognizing fellow-perceivers, including God the great perceiver. Immanuel Kant reduces the self-other relation to a subject/object relation, and so on. The point of all of this is simply to indicate that a good deal of our philosophic tradition has been predicated on immediacy. This quest for certainty in the philosophic tradition comes as no surprise. It is important to realize, however, the various ways in which one can look for certainty. At different times people have looked for certainty in terms of the past, or tradition, or authority. At other times certainty has been identified with the future, in terms of an afterlife or a determinate view of history, or the view that the end justifies the means. While these two approaches have been noticed before, it is important now to realize how committed philosophy has been to the quest for certainty in terms of the present qua immediate.

In our century, the phenomenologist Alfred Schutz has described the commonsense world, or the world of everyday life, as one of social action. It is a world of typification wherein each person interprets his or her situation in terms of needs, hopes, or motives, but does so within a biographical situation where intersubjectivity is taken for granted. The everyday world is one wherein interpretations arise from previous shared experiences: our own, our parents', our teachers', and so forth.

> To the natural attitude the world is not and never has been a mere aggregate of colored spots, incoherent noises, centers of warmth and cold. Philosophical or psychologi-

cal analysis of the constitution of our experiences may afterwards, retrospectively, describe how elements of this world affect our senses, how we passively perceive them in an indistinct and confused way, how by active apperception our mind singles out certain features from the perceptional field, conceiving them as well delineated things which stand out over against a more or less unarticulated background or horizon. The natural attitude does not know these problems. To it the world is from the outset not the private world of the single individual but an intersubjective world, common to all of us, in which we have not a theoretical but an eminently practical interest. The world of everyday life is the scene and also the object of our actions and interactions.[19]

In such a world, wherein knowledge is socially derived, the "typifying medium *par excellence* . . . is the vocabulary and the syntax of everyday language."[20] In short, in the realm of the natural attitude, intersubjectivity is assumed as a given. It is rather in philosophy proper that the question of the grounds for assuming intersubjectivity arises. As Maurice Natanson has put it, recognizing "that it is a decisive feature of daily life that the problem of intersubjectivity does not arise as a formal issue, we may still say that it is part of the task of philosophy to account for this state of affairs as well as to go on to develop the methodological principles underlying relationships between persons."[21] Anything approaching an adequate account of Schutz's position is beyond the scope of this chapter; I refer to Schutz to bring out a point, or rather a curiosity. For Schutz, the intersubjectivity of the situation is already given in ordinary day-to-day affairs. I find myself involved in the intersubjective pragmatic world of "typicality." I am consistently involved with other people in terms of typifying their activity to myself. I assume that I know, or can know, what they mean by such and such an action, and vice versa. But if the commentators referred to at the beginning of this chapter are even somewhat correct (Slater, Roszak, Bellah et al., Campbell), we are confronted by a new sedimentation. Not only does the problem of the other arise at the philosophic level as the "other experienced as absent," as "not me" via imaginative variation; the other is now no longer to be taken for granted at the experiential level of everyday life, because everyday life is now dominated by immediacy. Hence, in some way empathy, as a derivative form of intersubjectivity, will appear not only as an epistemic problem on the philosophical level, but as an ontological problem on the "existential" level.

Thus far we have examined two of James's three levels: namely, common sense and philosophy. While agreeing with Schutz on the way intersubjectivity arises as a problem, we have seen reasons also to retain James's "suspicion of common sense." In this case, the suspicion took the form of not taking intersubjectivity for granted at the commonsense level. Let us next look at the level of science, and specifically at the question of medicine as a science and the role immediacy plays here.

Medicine and Immediacy

This same fixation with immediacy can be found in medicine. This is not surprising, since however one interprets the situation, there is some interplay among medicine, the everyday world, and philosophical systems. To see the importance of immediacy, we need only raise the question, Is medicine an art or a science? The attempt to reify the doctor-patient relationship, to reduce the patient to a disease, is a clear case of moving from the contextual to the immediately self-evident. But as H. Tristram Engelhardt and others have pointed out, often the symptoms a patient has can be "explained" by subsumption under several competing "covering law" models.

> The multiple factors in such well-established diseases as coronary artery disease suggest that the disease could

167

be alternatively construed as a genetic, metabolic, anatomic, psychological, or sociological disease, depending on whether one was a geneticist, an internist, a surgeon, a psychiatrist, or a public health official. The construal would depend upon the particular scientist's appraisal of which etiological variables were most amenable to his manipulations.[22]

In short, the diseased patient cannot and should not be universally defined. The patient's plight cannot be reduced to an immediate self-evident situation, one whose solution is "known in advance." Engelhardt sees a "shift in nosology . . . back to a 'Hippocratic' notion of disease in the sense of a . . . contextual concept."[23] To the extent that this trend is continued, medicine would be seen as something partially vague or mysterious, in which diseases "such as cancer, tuberculosis, and schizophrenia . . . exist, but as patterns of explanation, not as things in themselves or as eiditic types of phenomena."[24] But there remains the eternal temptation to view medicine as a science possessed with some immediately self-evident concepts. Consider, for example, the demand for a precise operational definition of death for purposes of organ transplant. Hans Jonas has charged that the predominant motivation behind such attempts is to turn a vague, contextual situation into one that is immediately self-evident.

We do not know with certainty the borderline between life and death, and a definition cannot substitute for knowledge. . . . In this state of marginal ignorance and doubt the only course to take is to lean over backward toward the side of possible life. It follows that interventions [for transplant purposes] . . . should be regarded on a par with vivisection and on no account be performed on a human body in that equivocal or threshold condition. And the definition that allows them, by stamping as unequivocal what at best is equivocal, must be rejected.[25]

In sum, immediacy, defined as the opposite of the vague or the mysterious, has become a threat to the everyday world, the world of medicine, and the world of philosophy, although the issue does not appear in exactly the same form in each of the three domains. Immediacy is more an epistemic desideratum on the philosophical and scientific levels; but it has ontological aspects on the level of common sense—to the extent that the world of common sense is not itself viewed as an intellectual construct, pointing beyond itself to something "more."

Further, the whole issue of empathy appears as a problem precisely to the extent that immediacy predominates. That is, we tend to reify the contextual situation to the extent that "the other" appears as a problem, as something to be attained. This position assumes that what is immediately available is the world of the egoic, the "owned world," and that via empathy one can act *as if* one were looking at matters through the eyes of the other, which by definition one is not doing, since the other qua alter ego is not immediately given. The situation is further complicated by the fact that the egoic is unconsciously assumed in the everyday world of common sense. One uncritically assumes the wrap-around space of Slater, the "in here" position of Roszak, and so on.

My opposing position holds that the self is not immediately given, either epistemically or ontologically. That is, at the primordial level of experience, one does not find the consciousness/content distinction or the self/other distinction as already drawn. This distinction arises retrospectively, though once drawn, it is "informing," but not sufficient or primary. Moreover, the distinction is contextual, varying from situation to situation. If this is correct, empathy will appear as a not-to-be-completely-grounded phenomenon, epistemically speaking, and as a situation compelling action, ontologically speaking.

Since this assertion of the importance of vagueness stems from James, let us briefly review his views on language, metaphysics, and the affective domains in human life.

James on Language and Metaphysics

We have seen that, while James wrote no complete treatise on language, his writings do reveal a multidimensional approach toward language and its relationship to reality. Specifically, James sometimes felt that language insulates us from reality. But he also at least sometimes recognized the necessity of language and suggested how it might be more adequately employed. Finally, there exist texts where James indicates that language can touch the surface of reality but cannot plumb its depths.[26] What is important here is the clear realization that discourse, while necessary, cannot contain the whole of reality. And this is so regardless of what level or type of reality one is considering. For this reason, empathy as an epistemic issue will appear as incomplete, and essentially so. More positively stated, empathy presupposes an open-textured or vague situation. Ontologically, empathy is performative, and as such again it reaffirms the indeterminate.

This view of the possibilities for as well as the limitations within language is reflected in James's radical empiricism. For James, reality is richer, more abundant, than is usually thought. In his relational metaphysic, consciousness is rejected as a substance, but functionally defined as the most intimate type of conjunctive relation. Consciousness of self, like consciousness of any other object-for-consciousness, is available only retrospectively. Going further, if a given moment of experience can be counted twice over as it disappears into the past, then there is no reason why it cannot be counted three or four times over, for example, as the object for an alter ego. Experience

> in its original immediacy is not aware of itself, it simply *is,* and the second experience is required for what we call awareness of it to occur. . . . Granting . . . that [experience] can appear in the successions that I have so schematically described, . . . there is . . . nothing absurd in the notion

of its being felt in two different ways at once, as yours, namely, and as mine. It is, indeed, "mine" only as it is felt as mine, and "yours" only as it is felt as yours. But it is felt as neither *by itself,* but only when "owned" by our two several remembering experiences, just as one undivided estate is owned by several heirs.[27]

In this outlook, reality is not owned by anyone—either the ego or the alter ego. Such descriptions of reality are the result of consequent additions to the primary world of pure experience. Neither the self nor the alter ego is primordially given qua distinct entity. As Myers has noted, at the primordial level, for James, "the self was the ultimate mystery;"[28] and again, "the metaphysical dimensions of the self surmount the understanding."[29] Consciousness, as pure intention, has come on the scene, so to speak. It has arisen; but once it does arise, it exhibits a curious stubbornness; it cannot simply be done away with, omitted, or ignored. This is so, whether one is speaking of one's own consciousness or the awareness of the alter ego. Both are, qua distinct, derivative experiences. I do not find myself, at the primordial level of experience, aware of myself as a consciousness distinct from its object. Nor do I find an alter ego for whom there is a world like mine. These distinctions arise retrospectively, through the matrix of language. For James, the subject/object distinction arises when pure experience is *taken,* that is, talked of, twice. It is through language that the consciousness/content distinction arises; and it is through language that the alter ego arises, and hence also the issue of intersubjectivity, and of empathy. Going further, once consciousness arises, either as owned or as consciousness of the alter ego, it cannot be subsequently reduced again to the realm prior to its arrival on the scene. Pure experience can grow by its edges, and some of these edges consist in the intimate conjunctive relations that constitute my consciousness, and also of the conjunctive and disjunctive relations that constitute the consciousness of the alter ego. It may be that the relations that constitute my consciousness can be more

171

easily articulated than the relations constituting the alter ego. But the important point is that neither is primordial; both arrive on the scene. In short, we now find ourselves embedded in consciousness, so to speak, both owned consciousness and the consciousness of the alter ego. And we do so precisely insofar as concepts and language have arisen. Having arisen, they must now be treated as a necessary but not sufficient dimension of reality.

In sum, James's metaphysics is quite consistent with his statements about language. The latter were ambivalent, suggesting ways in which language could be used in a liberating fashion to point beyond itself toward reality, but also suggesting that language leaves something out, that some dimension of reality escapes. When we apply this to the issue of intersubjectivity, and consequently to empathy, we realize the following: both the consciousness/content distinction and the owned/alter ego distinction arise retrospectively, through language. But once arisen, they cannot simply fade away. One has, in a sense, to work through the matrix of consciousness and of the alter ego toward the primordial. This is always only partially successful because the primordial grows by its edges, and these edges include consciousness and the alter ego together with his or her world.

The Affective as Vague

The world of common sense, insofar as it has become linguistified or infected by the worlds of science and philosophy, is itself only one "type" or "level" of reality. But reality contains more than the reflective, or more than the exclusively linguistic; it also contains a prereflective or "affective" dimension. This aspect of reality is an essential one, that is, it is not to be cleared up in the future. Finally, and most important, the affective dimension is essentially vague. In this sense, we might say that the affective dimension comes close to catching the basic feature of reality, namely, its ambiguity.

For James, those experiences that he terms *"appreciations . . .* form an ambiguous sphere of being, belonging with emotion on the one hand, and having objective 'value' on the other, yet seeming not quite inner nor quite outer."[30] An experience of a painful object is usually also a painful experience; a perception of loneliness is a lonely perception, and so on. "Sometimes the adjective wanders as if uncertain where to fix itself. Shall we speak of seductive visions or of visions of seductive things?"[31] As we have seen, each present moment in experience for James, as it drops into the past, is classified as consciousness or content, or both. The world of the affective or the prerational is more real *in the sense that* it preserves the original given vagueness of experience. "With the affectional experiences . . . the relatively 'pure' condition lasts. In practical life no urgent need has yet arisen for deciding whether to treat them as rigorously mental or as rigorously physical facts. So they remain equivocal; and, as the world goes, their equivocality is one of their great conveniences."[32]

For James, what is "present" at the most primordial level of experience is *not* immediate. Affectional experiences are more real than others to the extent that they preserve vagueness. Nevertheless, experiences do become classified as subjective or objective, conscious or content, mine or yours, and so on. These distinctions come on the scene; they are not primordial. They arise with and through language. The prereflective world, then, is not one where intersubjectivity arises as a problem.

At the affective level, the problem of empathy does not arise because the problem of intersubjectivity does not arise because the problem of own-ness does not arise. These are all retrospective. But once all of these do come on the scene, they are no longer reducible to "what was" prior to their arrival. As additions, they are real. At the prereflective level, vagueness is primordial. One must work through the encrustations of consciousness, intersubjectivity, and so forth, toward the affective, but the return is never complete. The affective cannot be ignored or explained away. Furthermore, there is no nonbiased division of the cognitive and the affective. Such a distinction would be itself a retrospective one.

The problem of empathy and intersubjectivity entered the world of common sense from the domains of philosophy and science. Both of these domains were reflections and perfections of questions a given culture asked of its environment. Our present modern world is bewitched by immediacy because that goal has been articulated and perfected by philosophy and science. In "infecting" the world of common sense with this project, philosophy and science change the world of common sense, so that it too becomes an intellectual construct, as opposed to lived experience. But as James saw, the influence was mutual. The original, vague amorphous world of common sense with its affective dimension renders the linguistic pronouncements of philosophy, of science, and *even* of common sense qua exclusive, merely formal abstractions. They give epistemic clarification, but they cannot plumb the depths of reality. Empathy appears as an epistemic issue because the possibility of the alter ego cannot be *immediately* grounded on the level of philosophy or of science. It is an ontological issue to the extent that the world of common sense is taken as the "really real" and is now bewitched by immediacy, by Slater's "toilet principle."

Empathy in Medicine

Physicians, from the perspective outlined above, find themselves encrusted twice over, so to speak. Consciousness has arisen, and also *professional* consciousness has arisen. From these encrustations physicians work back—not simply toward the world of common sense, but toward the prereflective or affective world. Such a recovery is never complete, and yet it must be attempted. Perhaps this is what modern medicine has in mind by the term "neutral empathy." Thus Herrman L. Blumgart, in "Medicine: The Art and the Science," carefully articulates both the disjunctive and the conjunctive transitions existing between doctor and patient. Quoting favorably Charles D. Aring, Blumgart asserts that

> "entering into the feelings of another and becoming similarly affected may not be the constructive method that has been supposed. . . . The physician able to determine his emotional boundaries, that is, where he leaves off and where someone else begins, and who does not indulge completely in the other's emotional problems, functions more usefully, happily, and gracefully." This attitude has been aptly denoted by the term "neutral empathy." "Compassionate detachment" is, perhaps, more precisely descriptive. One enters into the feelings of one's patient without losing an awareness of one's own separateness. *Appreciation* of another's feelings and his problems is quite different from *joining* in them.[33]

Here the alter ego appears as not completely grounded, epistemically speaking. I would, however, argue that the stance described as "neutral empathy" is itself an interpretative one, arrived at retrospectively. Doctors, embedded in professional consciousness, or "consciousness squared," work their way back toward the prereflective world, the affective. They do this by interpreting how they are like and how unlike the patient, that is, what disjunctive and conjunctive transitions are operative. But such an interpretation is already one step behind the lived world of ambiguity. In the prereflective world, a "feeling (of the patient's) pain" and a "painful feeling" are not yet distinguishable. Retrospectively, the event can be counted twice over, both in the consciousness of the doctor and as the patient's physical problem. So while the professional, qua embedded consciousness, must work toward recovery of the primordial level of experience, it is essential to realize that recoveries, that is, empathetic articulations, as partial, are essentially incomplete. Furthermore, they point beyond themselves toward a prereflective world, which is essentially vague, ontologically speaking. Since such analyses of the empathetic are incomplete, they compel action, pragmatically speaking. That is, they serve to point out once again that there is more to reality than the cognitive.

This same point concerning the alter ego as absent and empathy as epistemic construct is brought out by Richard McGraw's description of the medical student. In training, the nascent physician is exposed to a graduated continuum of "patient models." This succession of models becomes part of the physician's "sedimented" experience. "The first 'patient' the student is introduced to is the cadaver. The cadaver is obviously a highly complex model for the beginning student, yet understanding the cadaver is often easier than trying to understand the living, responding, feeling persons whom the student will ultimately meet and work with when he becomes a practitioner." [34]

After the "cadavers" the student is exposed to so-called "heart-lung preparations," then to "specimens of blood and urine." The net result of such a learning process is that "the first human patients the student examines in his physical diagnosis course and later talks to are in a sense functioning as manikins for him. His interaction with them is quite perfunctory." [35] It is hoped, however, that the student moves from this mechanistic stage to the level of understanding more and more of the "social symbiosis of the patient's real life." As McGraw puts it, "In clinical work the student moves progressively from perceiving or diagnosing his patient as a case of pneumonia (no small feat in itself) to understanding him in human terms—first as a feeling human being and then as a part in a complex fabric or network of family, marital, social, and occupational contexts." [36]

Here, as in the case of neutral empathy, the doctor must work backward, so to speak. Empathy has arisen as a goal precisely because consciousness and then scientific consciousness have come on the scene. The new doctors work their way through the manikins or models toward the primordial experiences they have re-ified. Such recoveries are, again, incomplete, since the patient is being viewed through the *model* of the cadaver, or what not. Epistemically, I cannot completely ground the alter ego. Neverthe-less, the incompleteness of the epistemic argument points, I would argue, toward the ontological need for acting.

In both the domain of medicine and that of philosophy, em-pathy exists as a problem or goal because pure consciousness has come on the scene as a "rip" or "tear," in Sartrean terminology. The very incompleteness of the epistemic argument for empathy serves as an indication of the need for action. But in addition, it serves to remind us that, at the primordial level, reality is vague, ambiguous, incomplete, and essentially so.

Conclusion

I have now described in some detail how empathy has become an issue. The everyday world once took the alter ego for granted; in such an intersubjective world, there was no reason to act *as if* one were in the other's shoes. But the everyday world has now itself been infiltrated by the values of immediacy and self-evidence, stemming from the world views of science and philosophy. These two areas did not create these norms, but did idealize and perfect them, to the extent that they return to the everyday world in an extremely reinforced position. Because of this, the everyday world in a sense no longer exists in its primordial, prereflective form. The everyday world is now itself a conceptual paradigm, insofar as it clearly espouses immediacy as optimal. At the very least, the original vagueness of the everyday world is in danger of being lost and of being replaced by conceptual analysis.

My initial quotation alluded to different types of reality, de-scribed through language, and to James's refusal to set up any one type as definitive. There is an incompleteness to all levels of explanation; reality is richer, that is, more *vague* than any conceptualization, or indeed, richer than all conceptualizations added together.

Empathy now can arise as a *descriptive* problematic on any of three levels, because each of these levels is now linguistic. But language, as James showed, is a two-edged sword; it can liberate, but it can also insulate. Language is now necessary; like consciousness, it is something in which we are "embedded." James recognized the need for language, but he also remained suspicious of it. Ultimately, for him, the reality could not be completely "named" or "described." When one attempts to describe and ground the relationship of one ego to another, essential incompleteness is the result, because such descriptions are already retrospective. Said differently, at the prereflective or primordial level, this distinction of ego and alter ego is not *immediately* given. What is present at the most primordial level is not self-evident; it is vague, amorphous, ambiguous. Consciousness *becomes* owned. Insofar as consciousness of various types has evolved, even within a single self, empathy can arise as a problem. In this sense, descriptive attempts to ground the relationship of ego to the alter ego are unavoidable, though ultimately, not completely available. Once the worlds of science and philosophy have arisen, they are not reducible—one cannot simply return to the world of common sense. Hence empathy as a problem is doomed to incompleteness on the epistemic level. While such a conclusion might initially seem disconcerting, the burden of this chapter has been to suggest an alternative interpretation. First, the incompleteness is not bad, unless one presupposes immediacy and certainty as normal. Second, given a Jamesian relational metaphysics, the universe is essentially incomplete, and in that sense *vague*. Ontologically, in such a universe empathy qua incomplete demands action. The *idea* of empathy is not empathizing, and for the pragmatist, there is something to the notion that at least part of the proof of the pudding is in the eating. Empathy became an epistemic problem through philosophy and science. But empathy became an ontological issue when the reality was taken as clear and distinct, or as immediately given, finished. The purpose of this chapter and, indeed, of this book in general has been to show that such a view of reality is a mistake, or more positively said, to assert that vagueness is not, ontologically speaking, a fall from grace.

(Non)Conclusion

Life as a "Real Fight";
Text as "Spur"

The foregoing chapters have consistently argued for the importance of "the vague" in any understanding of the works of William James. Our reflections were of three types: "Interpretations," "Conversations," and "Applications." In none of these areas has a claim been made for either completeness or objectivity. Indeed, the claim that objectivity can be attained has been specifically rejected. Rather has the attempt been made to "privilege" one concept, "the vague," with its implications about the limitations of language, and to show how an interesting approach to James can be undertaken through this "symbol."

Part One, "Interpretations," commenced with an exposition of the similarities to be found in at least some parts of *The Principles* and *The Varieties*. Though ostensively about different subjects, namely, science and religion, these two texts have much in common. (Indeed, James even talks longingly about a "science of religion" in *The Varieties*.) The accounts offered in these two texts are comparatively descriptive in nature, revealing that James thought the features of both science and religious experience accessible; the phenomena being studied were, or at least could be, "present." Going further, one can see definite affinities between "the vague" as it is used in *The Principles* and "the more" in *The*

Varieties. Both are "concepts" that emphasize the fringe, the edge of experience, the ever-not-quite, and so forth. Both texts emphasize the richness of experience and the need for zest and intensity. In short, *The Principles* affirms consciousness as a focus/fringe continuum, and James, acting as a psychologist, found religious experience dealing with that very same issue.

Further, both these texts contain the seeds of their own undermining. In *The Principles*, James viewed consciousness as both selective and intentional, and such a "picture" will ultimately preclude a completely descriptive account. The briefer version of his *Psychology* will prove even more troublesome, reaffirming the importance of that which cannot be spoken about—the "inarticulate." The comparative problem in *The Varieties* concerns James's emphasis on religious experience as concerned with individualized feeling—where we "catch real fact in the making."[1] But *do* we "catch" it? James's comments about language show the incipient difficulty of the situation: "Compared with this world of living individualized feelings, the world of generalized objects which the intellect contemplates is without solidity or life. As in stereoscopic or kinetoscopic pictures seen outside the instrument, the third dimension, the movement, the vital element, are not there. We get a beautiful picture of an express train supposed to be moving, but where in the picture, as I have heard a friend say, is the energy or the fifty miles an hour?"[2] This text is interesting, not only for its continued use of simile and analogy, but for the possibility it raises of an infinite regress. If James cannot show how to use language positively, or show how to discard it, he cannot make the religious experience "present." He will become more and more troubled with language.

Whatever positivistic tendencies exist in *The Principles*, and they do exist, by the time of *Pragmatism* James is clearly worried about being taken as a positivist, that is, of offering up a methodology that did not allow religion to be taken as a meaningful (true) experience. This was a major theme of Chapter Two, wherein it became clearer that James will give up any view of reality as completely logical, either now or in the future, rather than dismiss the validity of the religious experience. In this sense, it is his religious stance that prompts a rejection of positivism as much as anything else. In this context we must recall that *Pragmatism* is offered as a mediator, that is, not as an advocate of science over religion. Further, the "corridor" image of the pragmatic method offered there is misleading—to the extent that it intimates descriptive neutrality.

The issues of science and religion were never far apart from each other in James's mind. One was, so to speak, defined in terms of the other—or one at least had its domain marked out by the other. By way of contrast, we might look at James's contemporary, Sigmund Freud. In an insightful work entitled *A Godless Jew*, Peter Gay argues that, "if Freud had been a believer like James, he would not have developed psychoanalysis."[3] That is, for Freud, the domains of science and religion are incompatible, and essentially so, and this very "fact" influenced Freud's view of science. Gay specifically contrasts the conflict model set up by Freud with the cooperative model advocated by James, and while admitting that it "is impossible to conjecture what kind of psychology James would have developed if he had been an atheist like Freud,"[4] nonetheless Gay does not hesitate to relate the issues in an overall fashion. "James the psychologist and James the philosopher . . . were at odds with each other. On the one hand, James recognized that science is bound to be irreverent. On the other hand, he was persuaded that reverence is necessary as a ladder to the most exalted truths. In the end, James's fascination with, and commitment to, religious experience gained the upper hand. . . . A little desperately, he resolved his urge toward faith by placing his bets on the will to believe."[5] Gay's analysis is astute in some ways, but it gives the impression or at least leaves open the possibility that there is a neutral endeavor termed "science," that the issue is that of science versus philosophy, and that religion and "reverence" are exclusively connected with the latter. On the contrary, I have argued that both science (psychology) and religious experience become problematized for James as his philosophy develops. Chapter Three argued that, overall, James viewed the scientist as an active participator in the creation of theories. "The Will to Believe" was ambivalent about the areas wherein personal preference was operative. James oscillated between identifying specific *content* areas or domains wherein subjective factors played a role, as opposed to identifying the criteria to be employed (i.e., forced, living, and momentous decisions between equally powerful hypotheses). The first of these two interpretations would curtail subjective elements to the seemingly soft areas of ethics, aesthetics, and religion. The second would view the difference between science and religion as one of degree rather than type.[6] James has often been read in the first way, especially when attempts are being made to bring out his affinities with, say, the analytic tradition, that is, to emphasize the descriptive dimension in his account of reality. But since James refuses to set up any one discipline, *including* science, as an impartial mirror of reality in *Pragmatism*, I would argue for the second of these interpretations. Similarly, Ellen Suckiel has argued that a

> promising instantiation of James's principle that faith is necessary for the evidence can be found in the context of empirical science. Some philosophers of science [Kuhn, Feyerabend] have argued, quite plausibly, that the acceptance of a scientific theory (at least provisionally and on some level) is necessary in order for evidence for that same theory to be collected. The point here, similar to the case of evidence for religious belief, is that the investigators' beliefs themselves determine how the facts shall be interpreted, and thus to that extent determine what the evidence is and what it means. Pre-evidential faith in the theory is necessary in order for confirmation of the theory to be possible.[7]

From this perspective, the difference between religion and science tends to become one of degree rather than one of kind.[8]

James kept trying to develop more of a cooperative than a conflict model concerning science and religion; "he never accepted
the conflicts between religion and science as permanent and irre-
solvable."[9] Eugene Fontinell believes that "as his [James's] metaphysics slowly took form, a more harmonious relation between
science and religion was increasingly suggested. . . . Both in our
moral and in our religious life—indeed even to a degree in our
scientific life—James insisted upon the necessity of beliefs or faith
commitments. . . ."[10]

From our perspective, then, description ultimately gives way
to direction in James's outlook, as his thought develops. This is
made apparent in Chapters Two, Three, and Four, in different
ways. James's metaphysical position in A Pluralistic Universe is
not neutral, but is rather presented as a form of pluralistic pantheism. More important, it becomes apparent that *any* metaphysical outlook involves an element of preference, including those
purporting to be naturalistic or scientific in form. James's views
of language, and especially of logic as an ideal language form,
constitute the pivotal point of this development. I have argued
for a realist interpretation of his notion of "pure experience,"
akin to Tillich's notion of "symbol."[11] His view of metaphysics,
as presented in A Pluralistic Universe, points beyond itself, so to
speak. Language does not go all the way down; yet James seems
to have more and more difficulty alluding to what is beyond it, or
alternatively, simply discarding language.

In short, James's realization that his description of consciousness was inadequate prompted him to develop a more hermeneutic
approach to both the self and reality, one wherein language was
necessary but insufficient, one wherein recovery was possible but
always partial. Even here, there remains the constant threat of the
inarticulate. But James's views on religious experience, as they
develop, tempt him to suggest/believe that one can stop using language and act, that is, that language is not necessary. Two things
render this development problematic; first, James had in several
texts indicated that language, and concepts, had a necessary role
to play. This, admittedly, one might simply change one's mind

about. But second, James himself does not stop talking, or writing, for that matter. This is the crux of the issue.

On one level, it is true that, when James does talk, his texts undermine themselves for the reader. That is, they are directional, or they point beyond themselves. They are no longer descriptive— or at least not exclusively so. Rather, James's texts are a "spur" in the Nietzschean sense of that term.[12] This is the James we are familiar with, telling us that "the proof of the pudding is in the eating," urging us to try out ideas as plans of action, and so on. This is the more "existential" side of James, reminding us that life is a real fight, or at least that it feels like a real fight, that the "idea" or "concept" of action is not action, and so forth.

This directional plea can be taken or appropriated in two different ways, and Parts Two and Three above are meant to bring out the two possibilities and the tension inherent therein. In actuality, James himself exists at the very edge of the "transition" between modernity and postmodernity. He is not, as I noted in the Introduction, exclusively a postmodernist. But the upshot of his *writing, as activity,* does bring him to the very edge of life being considered as a "text." Part Two, "Conversations," is a discussion among philosophers, or at least among their texts; it raises at the very beginning the issue of whether or not there is anything "outside" the text, that is, a *con*text, or whether all is conversation. Part Two proceeded in two ways. First, in conversation with other notable philosophers who had also given up the quest for certainty, it suggested that there was an existential or "will to believe" factor inherent in their respective philosophies, to a greater degree than any of the specific philosophers realized. Peirce, in developing over and against James, downplayed the affective and the irrational, and was somewhat "tenacious" in advocating the scientific method; Marx exercised the will to believe in a specific class, whose values he was, at least at times, willing to take as universal; Dewey exercised the will to believe in a process or method, whose outcome he associated with democracy. The point is that all three philosophers, or their respective texts, need to be viewed as directional, as projective rather than merely descriptive, as pointing back toward life. Accordingly, in a second way this part argued against Richard Rorty, saying that, at least in some sense for James, language does not go all the way down. There is, when one finishes the text, "something to be done"; all is not play; there is a tragic sense to life, and so on.

Part Three took this more existential dimension seriously, suggesting that language, as it becomes more and more sophisticated, can become a problem or barrier for the *activity* of empathy, that is, it oftentimes replaces the latter with empty concepts. Chapter Eight suggested that empathy can now appear on each of three levels as an opportunity or a challenge, as requiring a response on the part of the viewer-participator in the situation, and so on. Bewitchment with immediacy as a form of certainty was criticized for precluding one's ability to deal honestly with "the other" in empathetic situations. Finally, it was asserted that James's mature philosophy, wherein both the self and the other are not foundational but derivative, fragile, yet not reducible to the originary experience, might serve as a model for dealing more adequately with empathy as an issue. In a sense, then, this chapter was itself meant to be directional, in the form of an application to concrete situations. Chapter Seven, on modern art, suggested there were deep affinities between James's conceptual theories and another concrete area. In a Nietzschean sense, it argued for an aesthetic justification of reality [13] and suggested that we have much to learn from modern art in terms of giving up the quest for certainty, while not condoning a simplistic subjectivity. It affirmed the importance of process in art and in life as at least potentially liberating.

And yet, to come back toward Rorty a bit, we are faced with the fact that James does not stop writing, or talking, for that matter. He threatens to in *A Pluralistic Universe*, where he notes that, as long as one continues talking, intellectualism remains in possession of the field. But he goes on to say that he (James) *must* talk in order to deafen you (the reader) to talk. Or he must point,

point to the very "that" of life, and leave it to you the reader to decide. The pointing aspect of this is by now clear. I have argued that James's texts are inspirational and not merely descriptive; I have taken them as such and gone on to converse with other texts and to apply James's texts to other areas of experience. I would argue that James would want to be taken in this way, as a provocation,[14] so to speak. But what of his statement that he *has* to talk? And his statement that the sole purpose of such talk is to deafen? Is James being somewhat playful here? Is there another purpose? One possible response to the last query is to suggest that, for James, "keeping up the conversation was keeping the faith." Let us develop this theme in some detail.

In *Ariel and the Police*, Frank Lentricchia argues against those neopragmatists (e.g., Stanley Fish) who would do away with theory altogether, and he specifically uses James as his ally in the argument. Lentricchia says:

> My central point will be this: independently of Marx, and as the founding gesture of his work, James in effect accepts the most famous of Marx's theses on Feuerbach—that philosophy should be trying to change, not interpret, the world—but James out-Marxes Marx by saying that all the interpretative efforts of philosophy are always simultaneously efforts to work upon and work over things as they are. All intellectuals play social roles, whether they like it or not, James believed, because interpretation is always a form of intervention, a factor in social change or in social conservation.[15]

In a somewhat similar fashion, George Cotkin has argued that "the absolutely private James is only a reification, a fiction,"[16] and that "James consistently transformed his personal problems into public issues; he transcribed his own trying battles with doubt and depression into the text of his psychology and philosophy."[17]

As we have seen, however, James was sometimes tempted to

believe that he could cast off theory, or language, as if it were a coat, or have it removed as if it were an appendix. Progress toward reconciling the issue can be made by realizing that, overall, James's texts need to be viewed in three different ways. First, and most obvious, they need to be viewed as *descriptive*. James was certainly a master at this, oftentimes going for the jugular, so to speak, and accomplishing feats astonishing to those in other traditions (e.g., Husserl) who believed in the priority of a methodology. But James's genius for description also had its dangers, as we have seen in *The Principles* and *The Varieties*. As a result of this, James's texts need to be taken, second, as *directional*, as pointing beyond themselves toward at least a possible return to experience. The recovery may, indeed will, never be complete, since all *re*-covery is also a covering up, a re-*covery*. This is the more hermeneutic side of James's texts, wherein they serve as an invitation to the reader. As Emerson put it in "The American Scholar," "books are the best of things, well used; abused, among the worst. What is the right use? What is the one end, which all means go to effect? They are for nothing but to inspire."[18] Viewing James's texts as other than inspirational results in "vicious intellectualism," wherein language is taken as sufficient. Or worse, not viewing the texts as inspirational results in "neopragmatism," wherein theory is taken as superfluous and dispensable. I have argued that language, theory, concepts, and so on are necessary but not sufficient for James, while granting that language as such becomes more and more of a problematic, or more specifically, brings into question the availability or presence of that to which it is alluding. One major reason language becomes more and more of a problem is because there is a third sense to James's texts, wherein they are taken as his keeping up the conversation, that is, trying to say something new, relevant, inspirational, and so forth, not something "stale as a whale's breath," to use William Carlos Williams's apt phrase.[19] In "The Contingency of Selfhood," Richard Rorty makes a statement about Nietzsche and poetry (*widely* defined) that could equally well apply to William James:

"To fail as a poet—and thus, for Nietzsche, to fail as a human being—is to accept somebody else's description of oneself, to execute a previously prepared program, to write, at most, elegant variations on previously written poems."[20] And Charlene Haddock Seigfried has noted: "Plainly, James was most comfortable using language as a poet does, to create such a compelling interpretation of life that the reader can appropriate it as her own, rather than in using language as a logician does, to elaborate a consistent system and avoid errors of technique."[21] There *is* something outside the text in sense number two referred to above, but the text is also James's way of exercising the will to believe. Life is not reducible to writing for James, as it was, for example, for Franz Kafka.[22] But nonetheless, his text was his way of acting, of continuing the choice to continue made in 1868. In writing "The Will to Believe," James is exercising the will to believe. "Writing the text" is keeping the faith, so to speak. Gerald Myers has noted that, "even in advanced middle age, he [James] sometimes rose at 2:00 A.M. and wrote from 4:00 A.M. until dinner."[23] The writing of the text is, to a very significant degree, the creation of the fragile self—the "contingent" self. As Cotkin has argued:

> The personal resonance of James's discourse of heroism ... should not obscure, as he himself warned, the degree to which the need to create and to carry on despite obstructions, must "be conquered every minute afresh." Within this context, James's struggle to complete the "arch" of his philosophy partakes of the heroic. Moreover, in the context of his era's cultural and intellectual atmosphere, James's public philosophy figures as the "writing and rhetoric" designed to impel members of his audience who suffered from tedium or religious doubt to heroic acts, which were always weighted with responsibility and with awareness of the world's complexity.[24]

Myers combines "creativity" and "text as moral struggle" for James in the following reflective manner:

As many thinkers have testified, the value of philosophizing is as much in the process as in the product. It is an activity among activities, and like the others it can go well or badly. When it goes very well, it is as if thinking and living have merged into a single, harmonious, and vibrant process, as if thinking has found its goal in a newfound health of experiencing. James thought that a prolonged or chronic arrest or hesitation in thinking and living occurs at the onset of sickness or death; it is philosophy's mission to remove the blockage, to restore the fluency that is life itself. Composing his thoughts into linguistic pictures that imitate life's sensory flow was to seek the truth that paintings are said to have.[25]

For us, readers, "The Will to Believe," qua text, is a spur, a provocation to do something. As such, it does point beyond itself—even if only to another text. From James's perspective, however, the writing of "The Will to Believe," and of other texts, *is* the activity—or at least a very significant "part" of it. It is not a replacement for an activity. To assume so risks marginalizing language, or theory, to the status of being merely instrumental and ultimately dispensable—especially if the inspirational dimension is also ignored. That is, it would (incorrectly, I have argued) make of James a neopragmatist. It is here that Lentricchia is right. James did think there was "something to be done," something more than "giving oneself the illusion that one was doing something."[26] And his doing of it was the writing of the text. But the text, thus written, undermines itself by pointing beyond itself, that is, by serving as an inspiration to the reader.

Further, there are reasons why the texts are unfinished, reasons other than the fact that James simply did not have the time. As Seigfried notes, "it is profoundly fitting that James's last work is a fragment, prematurely cut off by his death."[27] James's texts were offered as a wedge back into the tissue of experience in sense number two above, but there is another sense in which text and experience begin to collapse for the author in this context. James is not simply describing what he sees, because he realizes more and more that language is not impartial—and yet it *seems* necessary. The issue of the return to personal experience becomes more and more problematized in the domain of "common sense" in Chapter Eight, above, as James realizes that common sense has been "infected" by language. "Pure experience" becomes more and more problematical as it becomes "impure experience," that is, experience infected by and only available through language. "Religion" as a personal experience becomes more unavailable as James tries to develop a "science of religion" in *The Varieties*, only to realize at the end that this science may declare personal experience outdated and insufficient. James's entire life was taken up with writing, speaking, and teaching, that is, primarily with texts. His writing may have suggested a return to experience, but for him, the writing *was* the return, the keeping up of the conversation because life felt like a real fight—one where there could be winners and losers. James's texts were the return; we need to "return from the return," in some fashion. One cannot relegate the return to a specific way, for the same reason that one cannot relegate the application of the will to believe to specific areas or domains, namely, there is no certainty given in advance.

James's texts constitute a form of rebellion, of protest or non-acceptance, and he writes "up-against-death" until almost the very end.[28] Daniel Bjork notes that, even as late as 1909, despite "the realization that he had to come to terms with the inevitability of suffering and death, James could not believe that infirmity precluded significant rejuvenation. As he experienced the fate of all flesh, something deep inside refused to accept it as natural. Creatively, however, he began to anticipate the end, began to see the limits rather than the possibilities of his intellectual efforts."[29] Here Bjork tends to ignore the importance of James's texts, or at least to focus on their cessation at the very end of James's life. Indeed, Bjork views James's attempts to deal with his heart condition during the last years of his life as "heroic and yet pathetic."[30] But he also astutely wonders aloud, in an almost Sartrean sense:

Did James avoid those physicians who would have confirmed somatic damage? To have known for sure would have been a great relief, but the knowledge would also have denied James his characteristic picture of the world. There would have been few alternatives, few experiments, few surprises. Such an outlook was not Jamesian, was not moral, was in fact un-American, for it would freeze experience into an unalterable predicament rather than allowing the individual the freedom to try a variety of provisional alternatives.[31]

While agreeing entirely with Bjork's interpretation here, I have been arguing that James's *texts* be taken in the same spirit, that is, as not neutral, as "not going gently into the night." James does keep talking and writing because writing, almost until the very end, is his activity, his life, his heroic struggle. His texts constitute a lifetime of keeping up the conversation in a context where, from the standpoint of the author, life "feels like a real fight." His texts constitute a spur, that is, an invitation to "overcome" them by going further, in application and in conversation. There is, then, still something "ineffable" or "inarticulate" about the texts written by James, something "more," in that they undermine themselves, indirectly disclose their own insufficiency, urge the reader to "surpass" them, and so on. In this final, or rather nonfinal, sense, James's texts are *vague*.[32]

Notes

Introduction

1. William James, *The Principles of Psychology* (New York: Dover Publications, 1950), vol. I, p. 254. Hereafter referred to as "PP."
2. William James, "The Will to Believe," in *The Will to Believe and Other Essays in Popular Philosophy* (New York: Longmans, Green and Co., 1927), p. 22. This essay collection is hereafter referred to as "WB."
3. William James, *Pragmatism* (New York: Longmans, Green and Co., 1908), p. 191. Hereafter referred to as "Prag."
4. Ibid., p. 194.
5. William James, *Essays in Radical Empiricism*, in *Essays in Radical Empiricism and A Pluralistic Universe* (Gloucester, Mass.: Peter Smith, 1967), p. 65. Hereafter referred to as "ERE."
6. William James, *A Pluralistic Universe*, in *Essays in Radical Empiricism and A Pluralistic Universe* (Gloucester, Mass.: Peter Smith, 1967), p. 60. Hereafter referred to as "PU." George Cotkin, in his recent book on James, argues that there is a political equivalent to vicious intellectualism: "Overconceptualization and vicious intellectualism represented the philosophical counterpart to the blindness of imperialism in the political sphere. Thus, the political and the philosophical were never far removed from each other in James's life or cultural perceptions" (*William James, Public Philosopher* [Baltimore: Johns Hopkins University Press, 1990], p. 143).
7. William James, *Psychology: Briefer Course* (New York: Henry Holt and Co., 1892), p. 165. Emphasis mine.
8. Eugene Fontinell, *Self, God, and Immortality: A Jamesian Investigation* (Philadelphia: Temple University Press, 1986), p. 64. James's difficulty in giving up language, in spite of its drawbacks, is taken up in the conclusion.
9. For the following, see Gabriel Marcel, *Being and Having: An Existentialist Diary* (New York: Harper and Row, Harper Torchbooks, 1965), pp. 100–121. See also Kenneth T. Gallagher, *The Philosophy of Knowledge* (New York: Sheed and Ward, 1964), pp. 236–50.

10. *Collected Papers of Charles Sanders Peirce*, vols. 1–6 edited by Charles Hartshorne and Paul Weiss; vols. 7–8 edited by Arthur Burks (Cambridge, Mass.: Harvard University Press, 1931–57), vol. 5, paragraphs 505–6.
11. WB, Preface, p. ix.
12. See ibid., and also James's statement about life "being or at least involving, a muddle and a struggle, with an 'ever not quite' to all our formulas, and novelty and possibility forever leaking in" (as cited in Ralph Barton Perry, *The Thought and Character of William James* [Boston: Little, Brown and Co., 1935], vol. II, p. 700. Hereafter referred to as "TCWJ.").
13. Frank Lentricchia, *Ariel and the Police: Michel Foucault, William James, Wallace Stevens* (Madison: University of Wisconsin Press, 1988), p. 125.
14. ERE, pp. 54–56.
15. Cotkin, *James, Public Philosopher*, p. 13.
16. Lentricchia, *Ariel and the Police*, p. 111.
17. Ibid.
18. Cornel West, *The American Evasion of Philosophy: A Genealogy of Pragmatism* (Madison: University of Wisconsin Press, 1989), p. 55. Emphasis mine.
19. *The Letters of William James*, edited by his son Henry James, (Boston: Atlantic Monthly Press, 1920), vol. I, pp. 95–96.
20. Ibid., vol. I, pp. 147–48. Brackets indicate that the manuscript is doubtful.
21. See TCWJ, vol. I, pp. 320–32. John J. McDermott, *The Writings of William James* (New York: Random House, Modern Library, 1968), pp. xxi–xxvi.
22. Gerald E. Myers, *William James: His Life and Thought* (New Haven: Yale University Press, 1986): "This case [i.e., of reading Renouvier] was not the only time that philosophizing helped James out of a depression; in fact, he continuously fought his emotional battles with thoughts and words, with philosophy. His was a talking cure, but of a different variety from the psychoanalysts" (p. 47). I return to the issues of words, i.e., of "text," below and in the Conclusion.
23. Daniel W. Bjork, *William James: The Center of His Vision* (New York: Columbia University Press, 1988), p. 240. In another section of the book Bjork states: "James endured a prolonged crisis between 1898 and 1910 that distressed him as much as his time of troubles as a young man—probably more" (p. 261).
24. Cushing Strout, "William James and the Twice-Born Sick Soul," *Daedalus* 97 (Summer 1968), p. 1069.

25. Bjork, *James: The Center of His Vision*, p. 243.

26. Strout, "James and the Twice-Born Sick Soul," p. 1073. Emphasis mine.

27. Bjork, *James: The Center of His Vision*, p. 244. Bjork goes on to say that the "will to believe was not enough" (p. 244).

28. Ibid., p. 268.

29. Charlene Haddock Seigfried also criticizes Bjork's position because it "makes of James a postmodernist"; but she does not emphasize the will to believe or the pervasiveness of religious experience in James to the extent that the present text does. See her insightful work *William James's Radical Reconstruction of Philosophy* (Albany: State University of New York Press, 1990), p. 3.

30. For an insightful analysis of the pervasiveness of the will to believe in James's overall philosophy, see Robert O'Connell, S.J., *William James on the Courage to Believe* (New York: Fordham University Press, 1984), chapter 6: "The Precursive Force of Over-beliefs."

31. Ellen Kappy Suckiel, *The Pragmatic Philosophy of William James* (Notre Dame, Ind.: University of Notre Dame Press, 1982), p. 14.

32. Fontinell, *Self, God, and Immortality*, p. 60. See also p. 155, where Fontinell says: "The human self emerges from fields designated 'physical,' but this self is neither identical with nor reducible to the physical fields from which it emerges and on which it presently depends." I discuss a version of this self in Chapter Eight, below.

33. Strout, "James and the Twice-Born Sick Soul," p. 1076.

34. Bjork, *James: The Center of His Vision*, p. 261.

35. For the notion of différance as both differentiation in space and also deferring or putting off in time, see Jacques Derrida, "Differance," in *Speech and Phenomena, and Other Essays in Husserl's Theory of Signs*, translated by David B. Allison (Evanston, Ill.: Northwestern University Press, 1973), pp. 129–60.

36. Seigfried, *James's Radical Reconstruction*, p. 13.

37. Ibid., pp. 13, 34.

38. William James, "The Sentiment of Rationality," in WB, p. 73.

39. Ibid., p. 72.

40. This major point is developed in a detailed and insightful manner by Seigfried in her text *James's Radical Reconstruction*.

41. Myers, *James: His Life and Thought*, p. xi.

Chapter One

1. William James, *A Pluralistic Universe*, in *Essays in Radical Empiricism and A Pluralistic Universe* (Gloucester, Mass.: Peter Smith,

1967), p. 256 (hereafter referred to as "PU"); William James, *Pragmatism* (New York: Longmans, Green and Co., 1908), p. 177 (hereafter referred to as "Prag."); William James, *Some Problems of Philosophy* (New York: Longmans, Green and Co., 1911), p. 82n (hereafter referred to as "SPP").

2. Prag., p. 191.
3. PU, p. 253; see also William James, *The Principles of Psychology* (New York: Dover Publications, 1950) (hereafter referred to as "PP"), vol. I, pp. 229–71.
4. PU, p. 286.
5. SPP, pp. 91, 127.
6. William James, *Essays in Radical Empiricism*, in *Essays in Radical Empiricism and A Pluralistic Universe* (Gloucester, Mass.: Peter Smith, 1967), p. 87. Hereafter referred to as "ERE."
7. ERE, p. 71; PP, vol. II, p. 320; Prag., p. 177; PU, pp. 287–89.
8. Prag., p. 148.
9. PP, vol. I, p. 453; vol. II, p. 579.
10. Ibid., vol. I, pp. 288, 139, 680–81.
11. Ibid., pp. 225, 424.
12. Ibid., vol. I, p. 515; vol. II, pp. 181, 335.
13. Ibid., vol. I, p. 453.
14. Ibid., vol. II, p. 296; see also William James, "The Will to Believe," in *The Will to Believe and Other Essays in Popular Philosophy* (New York: Longmans, Green and Co., 1927), pp. 1–31 (this volume hereafter referred to as "WB").
15. "The Will to Believe," in WB, p. 29; William James, "The Sentiment of Rationality," in WB, p. 91.
16. PP, vol. I, p. 142.
17. Ellen Kappy Suckiel, *The Pragmatic Philosophy of William James* (Notre Dame, Ind.: University of Notre Dame Press, 1982), p. 15.
18. Prag., p. 257.
19. It is, however, important to realize how seminal this chapter is for the work as a whole. Thus, for example, regarding consciousness as selective, Charlene Haddock Seigfried says, "The thesis of selective interest provides the structural framework for *Principles* and is developed in detail in chapters 1–2, 9, and 11–14 of the first volume and chapters 17, 19, 21–22, 26, and 28 of the second volume" (*William James's Radical Reconstruction of Philosophy* [Albany: State University of New York Press, 1990], p. 86).
20. See William James, *Psychology: Briefer Course* (New York: Henry Holt and Co., 1892), p. 152.

21. PP, vol. I, p. 225.
22. Ibid., p. 227.
23. Ibid., p. 218; see also p. 220 and vol. II, chapter 28, passim.
24. Ibid., vol. I, p. 461.
25. See ibid., vol. II, p. 336n; vol. I, p. 195n.
26. Ibid., vol. I, p. 196.
27. See Seigfried, *James's Radical Reconstruction*, chapter 7, passim.
28. PP, vol. I, pp. 284–85.
29. Ibid.
30. See ibid., vol. I, p. 240.
31. See ibid., p. 285.
32. Ibid., p. 139.
33. Jacques Barzun, "William James and the Clue of Art," in *The Energies of Art* (New York: Random House, Vintage Press, 1962), p. 320. See also Jacques Barzun, *A Stroll with William James* (New York: Harper and Row, 1983), pp. 45, 78, 101. Also see below, Chapter Seven.
34. PP, vol. I, p. 225.
35. Ibid., p. 234.
36. Ibid., p. 236.
37. Ibid., p. 240.
38. Ibid., p. 239.
39. Ibid., p. 245.
40. Ibid., pp. 255–57.
41. See ibid., p. 609.
42. Gerald E. Myers, *William James: His Life and Thought* (New Haven: Yale University Press, 1986), p. 82.
43. PP, vol. I, pp. 606–7.
44. Ibid., p. 254.
45. Myers, *James: His Life and Thought*, p. 447.
46. Ibid., p. 471. Myers specifically connects this preference for the *more* with the issue of immortality (p. 475). This theme is the subject of Eugene Fontinell's full-length study on James, *Self, God, and Immortality: A Jamesian Investigation* (Philadelphia: Temple University Press, 1986).
47. William James, *The Varieties of Religious Experience* (New York: Longmans, Green and Co., 1914), p. 26. Hereafter referred to as "VRE."
48. Ibid., p. 433.
49. Ibid., p. 455.
50. Ibid., p. 35.

51. Ibid., pp. 483–84.
52. Ibid., p. 508.
53. See Introduction, above.
54. VRE, p. 426.
55. Ibid., pp. 497–98.
56. Ibid., p. 459.
57. James, "The Will to Believe," in WB, p. 27. One could, of course, argue that, for many people who are not religious, the universe is also a "Thou."
58. VRE, p. 505.
59. Ibid., p. 209.
60. Ibid., p. 485.
61. Ibid., p. 358.
62. Ibid., p. 259.
63. See PP, vol. I, p. 310: "Our self feeling in this world depends entirely on what we *back* ourselves to be and do. It is determined by the ratio of our actualities to our supposed potentialities; a fraction of which our pretensions are the denominator and the numerator of our success: thus, Self-esteem=Success/Pretensions."
64. VRE, p. 41.
65. Ibid., pp. 526–27. The reference is to *Tertium Quid*, 1887, p. 99.

Chapter Two

1. Eugene Fontinell, *Self, God, and Immortality: A Jamesian Investigation* (Philadelphia: Temple University Press, 1986), p. 17.
2. See Arthur Burks, "Charles Sanders Peirce: Introduction," in *Classic American Philosophers*, edited by Max Fisch (New York: Appleton-Century-Crofts, 1951), pp. 41–53. In Chapter Five, below, I argue that in actuality there is a closer similarity between James and Peirce, at least concerning the necessity of the vague, and the affective dimension, than is usually admitted.
3. William James, *Pragmatism* (New York: Longmans, Green and Co., 1908), p. 78. Hereafter referred to as "Prag."
4. See ibid., pp. 103–23.
5. Ibid., p. 267.
6. Ellen Kappy Suckiel, *The Pragmatic Philosophy of William James* (Notre Dame, Ind.: Notre Dame University Press, 1982), p. 5.
7. Prag., p. 257.
8. Ibid., p. 266.
9. Ibid., p. 282.

10. Ibid., p. 88.
11. Ibid., p. 190; see Chapter Eight.
12. See, e.g., Prag., pp. 61–64.
13. Ibid., pp. 79–80.
14. Ibid., p. 283.
15. Ibid.
16. Ibid., pp. 283–84.
17. Ibid., pp. 290–91.
18. R. B. Braithwaite, "Laws of Nature and Causality," in *Readings in the Philosophy of Science*, edited by Baruch Brody (Englewood Cliffs, N.J.: Prentice Hall, 1970), p. 57. He defines a subjunctive conditional as follows: "We shall use the term *subjunctive conditional* for an assertion of the form: 'Although there are no A's, if there were to be any A's, all of them would be B's' " (ibid., p. 57).
19. See ibid., p. 57.
20. See ibid.
21. For an excellent analysis of Peirce's difficulties here, see John Smith, "Charles Sanders Peirce: Community and Reality," in *Themes in American Philosophy* (New York: Harper and Row, Harper Torchbooks, 1970), pp. 80–108.
22. Prag., p. 296.
23. Ibid., p. 287.
24. Ibid., pp. 288–89.
25. George Cotkin, *William James, Public Philosopher* (Baltimore: Johns Hopkins University Press, 1990), p. 170.
26. William James, *The Principles of Psychology* (New York: Dover Publications, 1950), vol. I, p. 254.
27. Cf. Burks, "Peirce," p. 113.
28. William James, *A Pluralistic Universe*, in *Essays in Radical Empiricism and A Pluralistic Universe* (Gloucester, Mass.: Peter Smith, 1967), p. 26. Hereafter referred to as "PU."
29. Ibid., p. 27.
30. See ibid., p. 31.
31. Ibid., p. 34.
32. Ibid., p. 35.
33. Ibid., p. 187.
34. Ibid., pp. 188–89.
35. Ibid., p. 192.
36. Ibid., p. 203.
37. Ibid., p. 8.
38. Ibid., p. 13.

39. Ibid., pp. 20–21.
40. Ibid., pp. 212–13.
41. Gerald E. Myers holds that by abandoning the logic of identity over the issue of whether experiences have parts, "James moved from being a psychologist to being a philosopher, and finally to being a mystic" (*William James: His Life and Thought* [New Haven: Yale University Press, 1986], p. 474). I reject this sequencing as too rigid in character; as early as "The Sentiment of Rationality," James tended to blur the distinctions between faith and reason.
42. PU, p. 218.
43. Ibid., p. 250.
44. Ibid., p. 257.
45. Ibid., p. 263.
46. Ibid., p. 290.
47. Ibid., pp. 310–11.
48. Ibid., p. 322.
49. See ibid., p. 318.
50. Ibid., p. 319.
51. Ibid., p. 325.
52. Ibid., p. 324.
53. Ibid., p. 328.
54. Ibid., pp. 328–29.
55. Ibid., pp. 317–18. See also Introduction, above, and Frank Lentricchia, *Ariel and the Police: Michel Foucault, William James, Wallace Stevens* (Madison: University of Wisconsin Press, 1988), pp. 103–33.

Chapter Three

1. This chapter concentrates primarily on the "internal" aspect of a Jamesian philosophy of science. The "external" aspect, i.e., the need to connect scientific procedure with ethical and religious dimensions in James, is by no means being disregarded here. I have concentrated on the structure of his philosophy of science to show that, even on this "internal" level, choices are necessary. I return to the connections between science and religion in the Conclusion, below.
2. For the following, see William James, *The Will to Believe and Other Essays in Popular Philsophy* (New York: Longmans, Green and Co., 1927), p. 249. Hereafter referred to as "WB."
3. For the following, see William James, *The Meaning of Truth* (New York: Longmans, Green and Co., 1909), p. 58. Hereafter referred to as "MT."

4. William James, *The Principles of Psychology* (New York: Dover Publications, 1950), vol. II, p. 667. Hereafter referred to as "PP."

5. WB, p. 108.

6. William James, *The Varieties of Religious Experience* (New York: Longmans, Green and Co., 1914), pp. 517–18.

7. PP, vol. II, p. 634.

8. WB, p. 68.

9. "Just as the physical sciences can give examples of different theories that equally explain the observed data, there are also divergent explanations for understanding the world as seen from different points of view, each consistent within itself and harmonious with the data. But these systems, equally satisfactory to purely logical analysis, still have to be accepted or rejected by our 'aesthetic and practical nature' " (Charlene Haddock Seigfried, *William James's Radical Reconstruction of Philosophy* [Albany: State University of New York Press, 1990], p. 35).

10. William James, *Pragmatism* (New York: Longmans, Green and Co., 1908), pp. 56–57. Hereafter referred to as "Prag."

11. WB, p. 67.

12. For the following, see ibid.

13. For the following, see Prag., p. 217.

14. MT, p. 60.

15. William James, *Some Problems of Philosophy* (New York: Longmans, Green and Co., 1911), p. 90 n. Hereafter referred to as "SPP."

16. For the following, see Prag., p. 216.

17. William James, *Essays in Radical Empiricism*, in *Essays in Radical Empiricism and a Pluralistic Universe* (Gloucester, Mass.: Peter Smith, 1967), pp. 68, 73. Hereafter referred to as "ERE."

18. Graham Bird, *William James* (London: Routledge and Kegan Paul, 1986), pp. 38–39; see also p. 71.

19. For the following, see SPP, pp. 70–71.

20. PP, vol. II, pp. 636–38.

21. See below, Chapter Eight.

22. PP, vol. I, p. 221.

23. Ibid., pp. 221–22.

24. Seigfried, *James's Radical Reconstruction*, p. 80. See also p. 101.

25. PP, vol. II, pp. 1–3.

26. Ibid.

27. SPP, p. 48n.

28. Ibid.

29. PP, vol. II, p. 2n.

30. Ibid., vol. I, pp. 606–7: this was also discussed above in Chapter One.
31. PP, vol. II, p. 76.
32. William James, *A Pluralistic Universe*, in *Essays in Radical Empiricism and A Pluralistic Universe* (Gloucester, Mass.: Peter Smith, 1967), p. 244. Hereafter referred to as "PU."
33. SPP, p. 82n. In the present chapter no analysis of the relation of perception and conception to the "object causing the perception" is given. The fact that consciousness is "intentional" for James in *The Principles*, however, and James's world of "pure experience" can both serve as indications that this distinction (perception/object of perception) is also relative. See below, Chapter Four.
34. See ibid., pp. 73–74.
35. Ibid., pp. 64–65.
36. PP, vol. II, p. 335.
37. ERE, p. 30.
38. SPP, p. 48.
39. PP, vol. II, p. 300.
40. SPP, p. 91.
41. Ibid., pp. 49–50.
42. Seigfried, *James's Radical Reconstruction*, p. 212. See, in connection with the present discussion of language, the whole of chapter 8, "Analogy and Metaphor."
43. PP, vol. I, p. 241.
44. Ibid., p. 245.
45. Ralph Barton Perry, *The Thought and Character of William James* (Boston: Little, Brown and Co., 1935), vol. II, p. 203.
46. *The Letters of William James*, edited by his son Henry James (Boston: Atlantic Monthly Press, 1920), vol. I, pp. 337–38.
47. Bird, *James*, p. 135. See also p. 77.
48. PP, vol. I, p. 444.
49. Ibid., p. 236.
50. Ibid., p. 472; see also Prag., p. 240: "The question 'what is *the* truth?' is no real question (being irrelative to all conditions) . . . the whole notion of *the* truth is an abstraction from the fact of truths in the plural, a mere useful summarizing phrase like *the* Latin Language or *the* Law."
51. Prag., pp. 132–48.
52. Ellen Kappy Suckiel, *The Pragmatic Philosophy of William James* (Notre Dame, Ind.: Notre Dame University Press, 1982), p. 43.
53. Prag., p. 213.
54. PP, vol. I, pp. 252–53.

55. Ibid., p. 280.
56. Ibid., pp. 264–65.
57. PU, p. 60.
58. Ibid., p. 324.
59. PP, vol. I, pp. 245–46.
60. ERE, p. 95.
61. PP, vol. I, p. 275.
62. For the concept of provocation as it applies to the pragmatists, see Cornel West, *The American Evasion of Philosophy: A Genealogy of Pragmatism* (Madison: University of Wisconsin Press, 1989). See, e.g., p. 54: "James is the exemplary Emersonian embodiment of intellectual power, provocation, and personality."

Chapter Four

1. A. J. Ayer, *The Origins of Pragmatism* (San Francisco: Freeman, Cooper and Co., 1968), pp. 224–42, 291–93. For an excellent criticism of Ayer's position, see Edward Madden and C. Chakrabarti, "James' 'Pure Experience' versus Ayer's 'Weak Phenomenalism,'" *Transactions of the Charles Sanders Peirce Society* 12, no. 1 (Winter 1976), pp. 3–17.
2. James Edie, in *William James: Essential Writings*, edited by Bruce Wilshire (New York: Harper and Row, Harper Torchbooks, 1971), p. xv.
3. Ellen Kappy Suckiel, *The Pragmatic Philosophy of William James* (Notre Dame, Ind.: Notre Dame University Press, 1982), p. 139. I will take up the problems with the world of common sense, as it becomes "infected" by language, in Chapter Eight, below.
4. Bruce Wilshire, *William James and Phenomenology: A Study of "The Principles of Psychology"* (Bloomington: Indiana University Press, 1968).
5. Richard Stevens, *James and Husserl: The Foundations of Meaning* (The Hague: Martinus Nijhoff, 1974).
6. See John J. McDermott, "The American Angle of Vision—I" and "The American Angle of Vision—II," *Cross Currents* 15 (Fall 1965), pp. 69–93, and (Winter 1965), pp. 433–60; also *The Culture of Experience: Philosophical Essays in the American Grain* (New York: New York University Press, 1976); and *Streams of Experience: Reflections on the History and Philosophy of American Culture* (Amherst: University of Massachusetts Press, 1986).
7. See above, Chapter Three.

8. William James, *The Meaning of Truth* (New York: Longmans, Green and Co., 1909), pp. xii–xiii. Hereafter referred to as "MT." See also William James, *Essays in Radical Empiricism*, in *Essays in Radical Empiricism and A Pluralistic Universe* (Gloucester, Mass.: Peter Smith, 1967), p. 160. Hereafter referred to as "ERE."

9. See ERE, p. 57: "Whenever certain intermediaries are given, such that, as they develop toward their terminus, there is experience from point to point of one direction followed, and finally of one process fulfilled, the result is that *their starting-point thereby becomes a knower and their terminus an object meant or known.*"

10. Ibid., p. 23.

11. William James, *Pragmatism* (New York: Longmans, Green and Co., 1908), p. 223. Hereafter referred to as "Prag."

12. ERE, p. 4.

13. Ibid., p. 160.

14. Ibid., p. 26.

15. See Prag., pp. 148–49.

16. The percept/concept distinction is particularly troublesome since James sometimes refers to reality *as* the "perceptual," even though in other places he says that reality *includes* the perceptual. See above, Chapter Two.

17. Ayer, *Origins of Pragmatism*, p. 318.

18. Ibid., pp. 322–23.

19. Ibid., pp. 191, pp. 323–24. More specifically, Ayer makes a threefold distinction. "The criteria by which we have to assess a belief which relates to a matter of empirical fact are different from those which apply to a belief which is concerned only with relations between ideas: and these are different again from the criteria which apply to beliefs whose function is to satisfy our moral and emotional requirements. These distinctions are implicit in James's writing, but he does not draw attention to them" (p. 191).

20. Prag., pp. 12–33.

21. Graham Bird, *William James* (London: Routledge and Kegan Paul, 1986), p. 42. See also pp. 5, 120.

22. See William James, *A Pluralistic Universe*, in *Essays in Radical Empiricism and A Pluralistic Universe* (Gloucester, Mass.: Peter Smith, 1967), p. 60 (hereafter referred to as "PU"); and above, Introduction.

23. Paul Tillich, *Dynamics of Faith* (New York: Harper and Row, 1957), p. 45.

24. Gerald E. Myers, *William James: His Life and Thought* (New Haven: Yale University Press, 1986), p. 318. It should be noted that Myers is

not entirely happy with James's position here. He goes on to say: "He [James] was painting verbal pictures. . . . [W]e should not expect more than broad brush strokes, bold analogies, suggestive metaphors, and arresting imagery. However, I do not intend to retract my . . . charge of implausibility" (p. 318).

25. ERE, p. 23.
26. Ibid., p. 92.
27. Ibid., p. 93.
28. See PU, pp. 282–83.
29. Eugene Fontinell, *Self, God, and Immortality: A Jamesian Investigation* (Philadelphia: Temple University Press, 1986), pp. 103–4. See also Fontinell's claim that "James came to realize that not everything in immediate experience was 'immediate' " (p. 108).
30. ERE, p. 93.
31. Ibid., p. 87. A similar statement could be made about identifying pure experience exclusively with the future.
32. Alfred North Whitehead, *Process and Reality* (New York: Harper and Row, Harper Torchbooks), pp. 27–29, 44–47.
33. ERE, p. 9.
34. Prag., p. 169. See also pp. 66–73.
35. PU, pp. 212–13; see above, Chapter Two.
36. PU, p. 249.
37. Ibid., p. 250.
38. Ibid., p. 290.
39. Martin Heidegger, "Letter on Humanism," in *Phenomenology and Existentialism*, edited by R. Zaner and D. Ihde (New York: G. P. Putnam's Sons, Capricorn Books, 1973), p. 148. See also p. 160.
40. See, for example, William James, *Some Problems of Philosophy* (New York: Longmans, Green and Co., 1911), pp. 97, 113.
41. MT, p. 42n. See also PU, pp. 339–43n.
42. MT, p. xii.
43. If James has a methodological postulate, it is that pure experience is not completely knowable—*not* that pure existence exists. See Chapter Five, below.
44. Prag., p. 190. See below, Chapter Eight.
45. Ibid., p. 191.
46. PU, p. 328.
47. Calvin O. Schrag, "Phenomenology, Ontology, and History in the Philosophy of Heidegger," in *Phenomenology*, edited by Joseph Kockelmans (Garden City, N.Y.: Doubleday and Co., 1967), p. 293.
48. See above, Chapter Two.

49. Ralph Barton Perry, *In the Spirit of William James* (Bloomington: Indiana University Press, 1958), pp. 106–8.
50. PU, p. 321.
51. Ibid., p. 330.
52. See ibid., pp. 328–29, and above, Chapter Two.
53. Gabriel Marcel, *Being and Having: An Existentialist Diary* (New York: Harper and Row, Harper Torchbooks, 1965), p. 96, and Introduction, above.
54. See the interesting discussion and comparison of James and Marcel on "the body" in Fontinell, *Self, God, and Immortality*, pp. 71–80.

Chapter Five

1. *Collected Papers of Charles Sanders Peirce*, vols. 1–6 edited by Charles Hartshorne and Paul Weiss; vols. 7–8 edited by Arthur Burks (Cambridge, Mass.: Harvard University Press, 1931–57), vol. 5, paragraph 400. All Peirce references are to this edition, as in "5.400" for volume 5, paragraph 400, etc.
2. See Carl Hempel, "The Theoretician's Dilemma," *Minnesota Studies in the Philosophy of Science: Vol. II: Concepts, Theories, and the Mind-Body Problem*, edited by H. Feigl, M. Scriven, and G. Maxwell (Minneapolis: University of Minnesota Press, 1958), pp. 37–98.
3. Peirce, *Collected Papers* 5.406.
4. Ibid., 5.453.
5. Ibid.
6. For an analysis of the problem here, see Rudolph Carnap, "Testability and Meaning," *Philosophy of Science* 3 (1936), pp. 420–68, and 4 (1937), pp. 1–40.
7. This same issue arises in other areas of Peirce's writings, e.g., in "critical common sense inquiry" vis-à-vis "scientific inquiry" and in "existential doubt" vis-à-vis "hypothetical doubt." See Peirce, *Collected Papers*, 1.75–76, 5.394.
8. Peirce, *Collected Papers*, 1.135–40.
9. See ibid., 5.408.
10. Ibid., 5.407.
11. For an excellent analysis of this issue in Peirce, see John E. Smith, "Charles S. Peirce: Community and Reality," in *Themes in American Philosophy* (New York: Harper and Row, Harper Torchbooks, 1976), pp. 80–108.
12. Arthur Burks, "Charles Sanders Peirce: Introduction," in *Classic American Philosophers*, edited by Max Fisch (New York: Appleton-Century-Crofts, 1951), p. 51.

13. Ibid., 51n.
14. Peirce, *Collected Papers*, 5.407.
15. Ibid., 7.187.
16. Ellen Suckiel makes a similar criticism of James, asserting that his view of the "absolutely true" as an "ideal vanishing point" does not, in her terms, "preserve the objectivity required of truth." "There is nothing self-contradictory about all persons agreeing to a proposition that is nevertheless false, even if its falsity were never discovered." *The Pragmatic Philosophy of William James* (Notre Dame, Ind.: Notre Dame University Press, 1982), p. 112. I disagree with this analysis, because I do not think that objectivity was James's sole or exclusive concern. Indeed, *Pragmatism* itself was offered as a mediator between the subjective and the objective.
17. Peirce, *Collected Papers*, 1.120.
18. Karl Popper, "Normal Science and Its Dangers," in *Criticism and the Growth of Knowledge*, edited by I. Lakatos and A. Musgrave (Cambridge: Cambridge University Press, 1970), p. 56.
19. Thomas Kuhn, "Reflections on My Critics," in *Criticism and the Growth of Knowledge*, edited by I. Lakatos and A. Musgrave (Cambridge: Cambridge University Press, 1970), p. 232.
20. Thomas Kuhn, "Logic of Discovery or Psychology of Research," in *Criticism and the Growth of Knowledge*, edited by I. Lakatos and A. Musgrave (Cambridge: Cambridge University Press, 1970), p. 6.
21. Thomas Kuhn, *The Structure of Scientific Revolutions* (Chicago: University of Chicago Press, 1962), p. 150.
22. Peirce, *Collected Papers*, 5.430.
23. See ibid., 5.358–87.
24. Graham Bird, *William James* (London: Routledge and Kegan Paul, 1986), p. 38.
25. See Peirce, *Collected Papers*, 5.466.
26. Ibid., 6.104.
27. Ibid., 5.119.
28. See, for example, ibid., 5.212, 5.536.
29. Ibid., 6.101.
30. Ibid., 6.295.
31. W. B. Gallie, *Peirce and Pragmatism* (New York: Dover Publications, 1966), p. 216.
32. John E. Smith, *Purpose and Thought: The Meaning of Pragmatism* (New Haven: Yale University Press, 1978), pp. 54–55.
33. Ibid., p. 55.
34. This does not necessarily mean that Smith would accept the position on Peirce advocated here.

Chapter Six

1. Karl-Otto Apel, *Charles S. Peirce, From Pragmatism to Pragmaticism*, translated by John Michael Krois (Amherst: University of Massachusetts Press, 1981), p. 1.
2. Ibid., p. 4.
3. William James, "The Sentiment of Rationality," in *The Will to Believe and Other Essays in Popular Philosophy* (New York: Longmans, Green and Co., 1927), p. 73. This volume is hereafter referred to as "WB."
4. Ibid., p. 92.
5. William James, "The Will to Believe," in WB, p. 11.
6. John Dewey, *Reconstruction in Philosophy* (Boston: Beacon Press, 1957), pp. v–vi.
7. John Dewey, "Context and Thought," in *On Experience, Nature, and Freedom*, edited by Richard Bernstein (New York: Bobbs-Merrill, 1960), p. 95.
8. See Richard Rorty, "Introduction: Pragmatism and Philosophy," in *Consequences of Pragmatism* (Minneapolis: University of Minnesota Press, 1982), pp. xiv–xvii.
9. John Dewey, "The Need for a Recovery of Philosophy," in *The Philosophy of John Dewey*, edited by John J. McDermott (New York: G. P. Putnam's Sons, Capricorn Books, 1973), vol. I, p. 95.
10. Ibid., p. 96.
11. For the following, see Dewey, *Reconstruction*, chapters 2, 3, passim.
12. Ibid., p. xxiii.
13. John Dewey, *Art as Experience* (New York: G. P. Putnam's Sons, Capricorn Books, 1958), p. 128.
14. John Dewey, "The Pattern of Inquiry," in *The Philosophy of John Dewey*, edited by John J. McDermott (New York: G. P. Putnam's Sons, Capricorn Books, 1973), vol. I, p. 226.
15. Ibid., p. 224.
16. Ibid., p. 225–26.
17. John E. Smith, *Purpose and Thought: The Meaning of Pragmatism* (New Haven: Yale University Press, 1978), p. 102.
18. Ibid., p. 109.
19. See Thomas Kuhn, *The Structure of Scientific Revolutions* (Chicago: University of Chicago Press, 1962), pp. 10–34, 92–110.
20. See ibid., p. 10.
21. See ibid., p. 151.
22. See above, Chapter Five.

23. Karl Marx, "Theses on Feuerbach," in *Karl Marx and Frederick Engels: Basic Writings on Politics and Philosophy*, edited by Lewis S. Feuer (New York: Doubleday and Co., Anchor Books, 1959), p. 245.

24. As quoted in Shlomo Avineri, *The Social and Political Thought of Karl Marx* (Cambridge: Cambridge University Press, 1968), p. 135. (Original source: *Rheinische Zeitung*, 14 July 1842).

25. Ibid.

26. Ibid., p. 136.

27. Marx, "Theses on Feuerbach," p. 243.

28. Karl Marx, "A Contribution to the Critique of Political Economy," in *Karl Marx and Frederick Engels: Basic Writings on Politics and Philosophy*, edited by Lewis S. Feuer (New York: Doubleday and Co., Anchor Books, 1959), p. 43.

29. Ibid.

30. Avineri, *Karl Marx*, pp. 68–71.

31. Ibid., p. 68.

32. Ibid., p. 72.

33. Ibid., pp. 74–75.

34. See above, Introduction.

35. *The Philosophy of John Dewey*, edited by John J. McDermott (New York: G. P. Putnam's Sons, Capricorn Books, 1973), vol. I, p. 267n.

36. For an explication of the term "quasi-chaos" in James, see Charlene Haddock Seigfried, *Chaos and Context: A Study in William James* (Athens: Ohio University Press, 1978), pp. 46–48.

37. William James, *Essays in Radical Empiricism*, in *Essays in Radical Empiricism and A Pluralistic Universe* (Gloucester, Mass.: Peter Smith, 1967), p. 87.

38. Avineri, *Karl Marx*, p. 69.

39. Tom W. Goff, *Marx and Mead: Contributions to a Sociology of Knowledge* (London: Routledge and Kegan Paul, 1980), p. 48.

40. Ibid., pp. 48–49.

41. For an excellent article contrasting Dewey and Marx on the issue of partisanship, see Alfonso J. Damico, "Dewey and Marx: On Partisanship and the Reconstruction of Society," *American Political Science Review* 75, no. 3 (1981), pp. 654–66.

42. For the debate between "critical Marxists" and "scientific Marxists," see Alvin W. Gouldner, *The Two Marxisms* (New York: Seabury Press, 1980), passim, but especially part 1.

43. See Apel, *Peirce*, pp. 195–96.

44. Jacques Derrida, "Structure, Sign, and Play in the Discourse of the Human Sciences," in *Writing and Difference*, translated with an

211

introduction by Alan Bass (Chicago: University of Chicago Press, 1978), p. 292.

45. Jacques Derrida, *Of Grammatology*, translated by Gayatri Chakravorty Spivak (Baltimore: Johns Hopkins University Press, 1974), p. 158.

46. Ibid., p. 167.

47. Jacques Derrida, *Speech and Phenomena, and Other Essays on Husserl's Theory of Signs*, translated by David B. Allison (Evanston, Ill.: Northwestern University Press, 1973), p. 156.

48. Richard Rorty, "Philosophy as a Kind of Writing: An Essay on Derrida," in *Consequences of Pragmatism*, p. 103.

49. Michael Ryan, *Marxism and Deconstruction* (Baltimore: Johns Hopkins University Press, 1982), p. 12.

50. Ibid., p. 21.

51. Ibid., p. 46.

52. Ibid., p. 47. The original reference is to the *Grundrisse* (London, 1973), 85, 106; 7, 26.

53. Ibid., p. 48.

54. Ibid., p. 83.

55. Ibid., p. 100.

56. Cf. ibid., p. 221.

57. Ibid., p. 38.

58. Ibid., p. 214.

59. Cf. ibid., p. 36.

60. For an expanded treatment of this theme, see my "James and Deconstruction: What Difference Does Différance Make?" *Soundings* 68, no. 4 (Winter 1985), pp. 537–59.

61. Richard Rorty, "Pragmatism, Relativism, and Irrationalism," in *Consequences of Pragmatism*, p. 164.

62. Richard Rorty, *Philosophy and the Mirror of Nature* (Princeton: Princeton University Press, 1979), p. 6.

63. Richard Rorty, "Philosophy in America Today," in *Consequences of Pragmatism*, pp. 213–14.

64. Richard Rorty, "Dewey's Metaphysics," in *Consequences of Pragmatism*, p. 73.

65. Ibid., p. 87.

66. Rorty, "Pragmatism," p. 166.

67. Ibid., p. 167.

68. Ibid., p. 172.

69. John Dewey, *Experience and Nature* (New York: Dover Publications, 1958), p. 40. Emphasis mine.

70. William James, *Pragmatism* (New York: Longman's, Green and Co., 1908), pp. 296–98. Hereafter referred to as "Prag."
71. Rorty, "Pragmatism," p. 174.
72. Prag., p. 295.
73. Richard Rorty, "Method, Social Science, and Social Hope," in *Consequences of Pragmatism*, p. 208.
74. Ibid., pp. 206–7.
75. Graham Bird, *William James* (London: Routledge and Kegan Paul, 1986), p. 154.
76. Rorty, "Introduction," p. xxi.
77. Ibid., p. xxx.
78. Charlene Haddock Seigfried, *William James's Radical Reconstruction of Philosophy* (Albany: State University of New York Press, 1990), p. 115. In the Conclusion, below, I indicate a sense in which Rorty has a point here, as author and text begin to collapse.
79. As quoted in Rorty, "Introduction," p. xxxi. Original source: Thomas Nagel, *Mortal Questions* (Cambridge: Cambridge University Press, 1979), p. xii.
80. William James, *The Principles of Psychology* (New York: Dover Publications, 1950), vol. I, p. 251.

Chapter Seven

1. Gay Wilson Allen, *William James* (New York: Viking Press, 1967), p. 187.
2. Ralph Barton Perry, *The Thought and Character of William James* (Boston: Little, Brown and Co., 1935), vol. II, p. 256.
3. See above, Chapter One.
4. W. Fleming, *Arts and Ideas* (New York: Holt, Rinehart and Winston, 1968), p. 513.
5. Alfred Neumeyer, *The Search for Meaning in Modern Art* (Englewood Cliffs, N.J.: Prentice Hall, 1964), p. 80.
6. Quoted in ibid. Original source: Juan Gris, "On the Possibilities of Painting," 1924.
7. Joseph-Émile Muller and Frank Elgar, *One Hundred Years of Modern Painting* (New York: Tudor Publishing Co., 1966), p. 18.
8. Ibid., p. 61.
9. Fleming, *Arts and Ideas*, p. 511.
10. Ibid., p. 513.
11. Neumeyer, *Search for Meaning*, p. 88.
12. Quoted in Muller and Elgar, *Modern Painting*, p. 94.

13. Fleming, *Arts and Ideas*, p. 517.
14. Neumeyer, *Search for Meaning*, p. 82. Original source: "Technical Manifesto of Futurist Painting, April 11, 1910."
15. Cf. Calvin Tomkins, *The Bride and the Bachelors*, Viking Compass edition (New York: Viking Press, 1968), p. 18.
16. Ibid., p. 33.
17. Marcel Duchamp, "The Creative Act," in *The New Art*, edited by Gregory Battcock (New York: E. P. Dutton and Co., 1966), pp. 25–26.
18. Calvin Tomkins, *The Bride and the Bachelors*, introduction by L. Meyer (New York: Viking Press, 1965), p. 5. All quotations other than this one are from the Viking Compass edition cited in note 15.
19. Quoted in Tomkins, *Bride*, Viking Compass edition, p. 2.
20. Alan Solomon, "The New Art," in *The New Art*, edited by Gregory Battcock (New York: E. P. Dutton and Co., 1966), p. 73.
21. See John Rublowsky, *Pop Art* (New York: Basic Books, 1965), p. 29.
22. Solomon, "New Art," p. 75.
23. For the following, see Rublowsky, *Pop Art*, p. 68.
24. Ibid.
25. Quoted in ibid., p. 70.
26. Neumeyer, *Search for Meaning*, p. 103. Original source: André Breton, *What Is Surrealism?* (London, 1936), p. 25.
27. Gillo Dorfles, "The Role of Motion in Our Visual Habits and Artistic Creation," in *The Nature and Art of Motion*, edited by Gyorgy Kepes (New York: George Braziller, 1965), p. 42.
28. Neumeyer, *Search for Meaning*, p. 131.
29. Allan Kaprow, "A Manifesto on Happenings," in *The American Experience: A Radical Reader*, edited by Harold Jaffee and John Tytell (New York: Harper and Row, 1970), p. 311.
30. Allan Kaprow, *Assemblage, Environments, and Happenings* (New York: Harry Abrams, 1965), p. 159.
31. See Roy Bongartz, "It's Called Earth Art—and Boulderdash," in *The New York Times Magazine*, February 1, 1970, pp. 16–30.
32. Kaprow, *Assemblage*, pp. 168–69.
33. John J. McDermott, "To Be Human Is To Humanize: A Radically Empirical Aesthetic," in *American Philosophy and the Future: Essays for a New Generation*, edited by Michael Novak (New York: Charles Scribner's Sons, 1968), p. 32.
34. The best aesthetic in these terms would be found in John Dewey, *Art as Experience* (New York: G. P. Putnam's Sons, Capricorn Books, 1958).

35. John J. McDermott, "Deprivation and Celebration: Suggestions for an Aesthetic Ecology," in *New Essays in Phenomenology*, edited by James Edie (Chicago: Quadrangle Books, 1969), p. 125.

36. Ibid., p. 128.

37. Amy Golden, "Sweet Mystery of Life," *Art News* 68, no. 3 (May 1969), p. 46.

Chapter Eight

1. William James, *Pragmatism* (New York: Longman's, Green and Co., 1908), pp. 188–91. See also Chapter Three, above.

2. The free play allowed to individual interests *within* a common conceptual scheme is brought out by Ellen Kappy Suckiel in *The Pragmatic Philosophy of William James* (Notre Dame, Ind.: Notre Dame University Press, 1982), p. 20. The issue that concerns us here, however, regarding the plurality of competing conceptual schemas, perhaps incommensurate, is not adequately addressed. Eugene Fontinell also finds this particular text important. Commenting on it, he says: "Such epistemological pluralism is, of course, a mode of perspectivism, but it is not—or at least not obviously—a mode of destructive relativism and superficial subjectivism" (*Self, God, and Immortality: A Jamesian Investigation* [Philadelphia: Temple University Press, 1986], p. 14). Fontinell catches more of the radical flavor of James's thought here.

3. See Alfred Schutz, *Collected Papers: Volume I, The Problem of Social Reality*, edited and introduced by Maurice Natanson (The Hague: Martinus Nijhoff, 1973), pp. 208–9.

4. Philip Slater, *The Pursuit of Loneliness: American Culture at the Breaking Point* (Boston: Beacon Press, 1970), p. 15.

5. Theodore Roszak, *The Making of a Counter Culture: Reflections on the Technocratic Society and Its Youthful Opposition* (New York: Doubleday and Co., Anchor Books, 1969), p. 252.

6. Ibid., p. 262.

7. Robert N. Bellah, Richard Madsen, William H. Sullivan, Ann Swidler, and Steven M. Tipton, *Habits of the Heart: Individualism and Commitment in American Life* (New York: Harper and Row, Perennial Library, 1986), p. 302.

8. Ibid., p. 296.

9. Ibid., pp. 300–301.

10. Ibid., p. 143.

11. Ibid., p. 295.

12. Joseph Campbell, *Myths to Live By* (New York: Viking Press, Bantam Books, 1973), p. 20.

13. *An Open Life: Joseph Campbell in Conversation with Michael Toms* (New York: Harper and Row, Perennial Library, 1990), p. 21.

14. Ibid., p. 35.

15. See Campbell, *Myths to Live By*, pp. 20–22.

16. Campbell, *An Open Life*, p. 21.

17. See Daniel Boorstin, "Is America Really Sick?" in *Reader's Digest* 97 (September 1970), pp. 92–94; condensed from *Newsweek* 76 (July 6, 1970).

18. See Harvey Cox, *The Feast of Fools: A Theological Essay on Festivity and Fantasy* (Cambridge, Mass.: Harvard University Press, 1969), passim.

19. Schutz, *Collected Papers: Vol. I*, pp. 208–9.

20. Ibid., p. 14.

21. Maurice Natanson, "Introduction," in ibid., p. xxxi.

22. H. Tristram Engelhardt, Jr., "The Concepts of Health and Disease," in *Evaluation and Explanation in the Biomedical Sciences*, edited by H. Tristram Engelhardt, Jr., and Stuart F. Spicker (Dordrecht: D. Reidel Publishing Co., 1975), p. 133.

23. Ibid., p. 133.

24. Ibid., p. 136.

25. Hans Jonas, "Against the Stream: Comments on the Definition and Redefinition of Death," in *Ethical Issues in Death and Dying*, edited by Tom L. Beauchamp and Seymour Perlin (Englewood Cliffs, N.J.: Prentice Hall, 1978), p. 57.

26. See above, Chapters Three and Four.

27. William James, *Essays in Radical Empiricism*, in *Essays in Radical Empiricism and A Pluralistic Universe* (Gloucester, Mass.: Peter Smith, 1967), pp. 132–33. Hereafter referred to as "ERE."

28. Gerald E. Myers, *William James: His Life and Thought* (New Haven: Yale University Press, 1986), p. 369. See also p. 348, where Myers asserts that for James the topic of the "self" was "philosophically opaque."

29. Ibid., p. 386.

30. ERE, p. 34.

31. Ibid., p. 35.

32. Ibid., p. 146.

33. Herrman L. Blumgart, M.D., "Medicine: The Art and the Science," in *Hippocrates Revisited*, edited by Roger J. Bulgar, M.D. (New York: Medcom Press, 1973), p. 38.

34. Richard McGraw, M.D., "Science and Humanism: Medicine and

Existential Anguish," in *Hippocrates Revisited*, edited by Roger J. Bulgar, M.D. (New York: Medcom Press, 1973), p. 48.
35. Ibid.
36. Ibid., p. 49.

(Non)Conclusion

1. William James, *The Varieties of Religious Experience* (New York: Longmans, Green and Co., 1914), p. 501.
2. Ibid., p. 502. See the similar difficulties brought up by James in *The Principles of Psychology* (New York: Dover Publications, 1950) concerning our lack of ability introspectively to catch the transitive parts of consciousness. He compares it to trying to catch a snow crystal in a warm hand to see what it looks like, or to our seizing a spinning top in order to catch its motion. See vol. I, p. 244.
3. Peter Gay, *A Godless Jew: Freud, Atheism, and the Making of Psychoanalysis* (New Haven: Yale University Press, 1987), p. 31.
4. Ibid., p. 30.
5. Ibid., pp. 29–30.
6. For a more extensive analysis of this issue, see my article "The 'Will to Believe' in Science and Religion," *International Journal for Philosophy of Religion* 15 (1984), pp. 139–48.
7. Ellen Kappy Suckiel, *The Pragmatic Philosophy of William James* (Notre Dame, Ind.: Notre Dame University Press, 1982), p. 85. Graham Bird has also criticized the sharp distinction between science and religion in "The Will to Believe," saying, "It is easy to imagine decisions in science which are in the ordinary sense both genuine and momentous" (*William James* [London: Routledge and Kegan Paul, 1986], p. 166).
8. As Graham Bird has noted: "James's philosophy not only covers issues in morality and religion, but was dominated by them. . . . Indeed, it is not too much to say that his epistemology was in part constructed *for* these issues. James evidently wished to provide an empiricism which was not only rigorous and down to earth but also accommodated moral, religious, even supernatural beliefs. It was this wish which led him to mediate between the tough- and tender-minded philosophies and to envisage with characteristic cheerfulness a new dawn in which empiricism and religion were reconciled and cooperative" (*James*, p. 144).
9. Eugene Fontinell, *Self, God, and Immortality: A Jamesian Investigation* (Philadelphia: Temple University Press, 1986), p. 113.
10. Ibid., p. 114.

11. See Chapter Four, above.

12. In *Thus Spoke Zarathustra*, for example, Zarathustra says, "Many die too late, and a few die too early. . . . Die at the right time— thus teaches Zarathustra. . . . I show you the death that consummates—a spur and a promise to the survivors." (*The Portable Nietzsche*, edited and translated by Walter Kaufmann [New York: Penguin Books, 1976], p. 183.) One dies at the right time when one's death serves as an inspiration. In a similar sense, one's text can serve as an invitation to be "overcome." For an excellent presentation and analysis of the issue of author, reality, and text, see Alexander Nehamas, *Nietzsche: Life as Literature* (Cambridge, Mass.: Harvard University Press, 1985).

13. In *The Birth of Tragedy*, Nietzsche says: "It is only as an *esthetic phenomenon* that existence and the world are eternally *justified*." See *The Philosophy of Nietzsche* (New York: Random House, Modern Library, 1954), p. 974.

14. On the general notion of "provocation" as it is found in James, Emerson, and other pragmatists, see Cornel West, *The American Evasion of Philosophy: A Genealogy of Pragmatism* (Madison: University of Wisconsin Press, 1989), passim, but especially pp. 54–68.

15. Frank Lentricchia, *Ariel and the Police: Michel Foucault, William James, Wallace Stevens* (Madison: University of Wisconsin Press, 1988), pp. 105–6.

16. George Cotkin, *William James, Public Philosopher* (Baltimore: Johns Hopkins University Press, 1990), p. 17.

17. Ibid., p. 64. Cotkin's emphasis is on the political aspect of this, while I am emphasizing the textual, though there is significant overlap.

18. Ralph Waldo Emerson, "The American Scholar," in *Selected Writings of Ralph Waldo Emerson*, edited and with a foreword by William H. Gilman (New York: New American Library, 1965), pp. 227–28.

19. See William Carlos Williams, *Paterson* (New York: New Directions Books, n.d.), p. 20.

20. Richard Rorty, "The Contingency of Selfhood," in *Contingency, Irony, and Solidarity* (Cambridge: Cambridge University Press, 1989), p. 28. Rorty defines "poet" in a broad generic sense, such that "Proust and Nabokov, Newton and Darwin, Hegel and Heidegger . . . fall under that term." Equally important for our purposes, Rorty continues by noting that "such people are also to be thought of as rebelling against 'death'—that is, against the failure to have created—more strongly than most of us" p. 24n).

21. Charlene Haddock Seigfried, *William James's Radical Reconstruction of Philosophy* (Albany: State University of New York Press, 1990), p. 210.
22. See Kafka's statement: "My life consists and always has consisted fundamentally of attempts at writing, and mainly of unsuccessful ones." Quoted in Anthony Thorlby, "Kafka and Language," in *The World of Franz Kafka*, edited by J. P. Stern (New York: Holt, Rinehart and Winston, 1980), p. 134.
23. Myers, *James: His Life and Thought*, p. 41.
24. Cotkin, *James, Public Philosopher*, p. 101.
25. Myers, *James: His Life and Thought*, p. 343.
26. See the opening line in Samuel Beckett's play *Waiting for Godot*, where Estragon says to Vladimir, "Nothing to be done," as well as his later statement to Vladimir that "we always find something . . . to give us the impression we exist" (Samuel Beckett, *Waiting for Godot* [New York: Grove Press, 1954], pp. 7, 44).
27. Seigfried, *James's Radical Reconstruction*, p. 394.
28. See note 14, above.
29. Daniel W. Bjork, *William James: The Center of His Vision* (New York: Columbia University Press, 1988), p. 256.
30. Ibid., p. 261.
31. Ibid., p. 262.
32. "With James's death, his particular sense of the unity of experience also dies, and we are left trying to patch back together its written fragments into a unified whole, a manifestly impossible task. But this Sisyphean task is one which we must ever take up anew in our human need to weave chaos into order, just as James did in his lifetime, and to which he invites us by the very shape of the fragment he bequeathed us." Seigfried, *James's Radical Reconstruction*, p. 395. I agree entirely with this point and have attempted to add one more, namely, a closer association between author and text in offering the invitation to the reader.

Index